Commendations for *This Light of Mine*

The world seems so weary, so wounded, so angry. Can followers of Jesus stem the tide of vitriol and pain? My friend Joe Stowell says we can. He reminds us of our high and holy call—to make a difference for good in an era so wrought with bad. I needed to read this book. I'm ready to let my light shine just a little brighter.

MAX LUCADO
Pastor, author, speaker

Joe Stowell has not only written a much-needed antidote for those Christians who think politics is the solution to the world's problems, but *This Light of Mine* also offers a way forward for those who already know better but don't know where to begin.

ROBERTA GREEN AHMANSON
Writer, speaker, philanthropist

Writing with a lightness of touch but without pulling his punches, Joe encourages us to take up the challenge of living attractive, gospel-shaped lives even as the winds of opposition blow strongly in our faces.

ALISTAIR BEGG
Pastor, author and Bible teacher on *Truth for Life*

People are not the enemy but the goal. The church is in great need of a different way to engage with Jesus to a non-Jesus world. Diving deeply into Scripture with a pastor's heart and a keen, sensitive eye, Joe Stowell calls the church to a better way to engage than being a shrill voice. Yes, the church is being marginalized and mocked, but so was Jesus. His way of reaching out and offering hope to those in spiritual need is still the way to go.

DARRELL L. BOCK
Executive Director for Cultural Engagement, Hendricks Center;
Senior Research Professor Theological
Seminary

This book is compelling and unapologetically countercultural, so refreshing. No matter who you are or what your political leanings are, you will feel convicted by this book. My friend Joe Stowell speaks from the Word of God: to some a stumbling stone but to us sanctuary. I pray that we will all be stirred into hope and action by the practical unfolding of the Christ-centered life to which Joe exhorts readers in this timely and important book.

BARRY H. COREY
President of Biola University and author of *Love Kindness: Discover the Power of a Forgotten Christian Virtue* and *Make the Most of It: A Guide to Loving Your College Years*

In a culture that has become largely hostile to biblical principles and long-cherished moral values, it can be challenging to know how we, as believers, are to conduct ourselves. That's why I'm so thankful that Joe Stowell has offered us a scriptural prescription for venturing into an increasingly dark society holding out the love and truth of Christ.

JIM DALY
President, Focus on the Family

This Light of Mine is refreshing, clarifying, convicting, and compellingly hope-filled. In these pages, my friend Joe Stowell takes us beyond a critique of the culture and the ways in which it is falling apart and points us to Jesus' plan. In Stowell's words, it is a plan for engaging the culture in ways that empowers the gospel and advances the kingdom. This indeed is God's plan for changing lives and influencing the culture. Joe, thank you so much for this gift of clarity during these confusing times.

CRAWFORD W. LORITTS JR.
Author, speaker, radio host; President, Beyond our Generation

The burden of this book is that we as believers might give a positive witness for Christ in our highly polarized and angry world. Joe warns that often the gospel is politicized, which becomes a stumbling block to many who are seeking for hope and forgiveness in our misguided culture. If you are looking for examples of how to represent Christ well without the self-righteous judgmentalism that some believers exhibit, read this book and then pass it along to a friend. And above all, let us be lights that point others to the light of the world!

ERWIN W. LUTZER
Pastor Emeritus, The Moody Church, Chicago

The dramatic downturn in our culture has left many followers of Christ confused about how to respond. Some have adopted a culture-warring mentality, while others have retreated into a holy huddle hoping for Christ's soon return. Unfortunately, neither of these responses are effective in attractively advancing the light of Jesus' kingdom into the darkness of our world. Thankfully, Joe Stowell has brought clarity to our confusion by showing us Jesus' way to influence an often-resistant culture for good and His glory. This compelling read is deeply scriptural and refreshingly practical. Thanks, Joe! We needed this.

ED STETZER
Dean of Talbot School of Theology

This Light of Mine is a courageous book for our time. As Christians grapple with the reality of living as people of the Way in a world that is growing increasingly secular, Joe Stowell powerfully calls us to live according to the foundational values of the kingdom of Jesus Christ. All of us would do well to examine our lives in light of this book so that the love of Christ may continue to flow through us into this hurting world. This book is biblically sound, theologically faithful, and pastorally wise. But what makes it compelling is the fact that Joe has precisely lived out in his life what he is calling us to do in this book.

FELIX THEONUGRAHA
President, Western Seminary, Holland, MI

The gospel of Christ is much more than receiving the salvation message and asking Jesus into your heart. The gospel is a way of life that makes a clear difference for Christ in your family, neighborhood, and community. My longtime friend Dr. Joe Stowell has written a practical and powerful guide to gospel-living in this book. Thank you, Joe, for showing us what it means to shake the salt and shine the light of Jesus wherever our sphere of influence may be!

JONI EARECKSON TADA
Joni and Friends International Disability Center

THIS

Living Like Jesus

LIGHT

in a Non-Jesus World

OF

JOSEPH M. STOWELL

MINE

MOODY PUBLISHERS

CHICAGO

© 2025 by
JOSEPH M. STOWELL

Scripture quotations are from the ESV® Bible (The Holy Bible, English Standard Version®), © 2001 by Crossway, a publishing ministry of Good News Publishers. Used by permission. All rights reserved. The ESV text may not be quoted in any publication made available to the public by a Creative Commons license. The ESV may not be translated in whole or in part into any other language.

All emphasis in Scripture has been added.
Edited by Pamela Joy Pugh
Interior design: Puckett Smartt
Cover design: Thinkpen Design
Cover graphic of dots light frame copyright © 2024 by Shutterstock AI Generator (2476170921). All rights reserved.
Author photo: Chris Segard

Library of Congress Cataloging-in-Publication Data

Names: Stowell, Joseph M., author.
Title: This light of mine : living like Jesus in a non-Jesus world / Joseph
   M. Stowell.
Description: Chicago : Moody Publishers, [2025] | Includes bibliographical
   references. | Summary: "Drawing from the Scriptures and the life of
   Jesus, Stowell provides a hope-filled, courageous response that empowers
   us to light up the darkness by living like Jesus in a non-Jesus world"--
   Provided by publisher.
Identifiers: LCCN 2024028587 (print) | LCCN 2024028588 (ebook) | ISBN
   9780802435316 | ISBN 9780802470430 (ebook)
Subjects: LCSH: Jesus Christ--Person and offices. | Bible. New Testament. |
   Christian life.
Classification: LCC BT203 .S7528 2025 (print) | LCC BT203 (ebook) | DDC
   248.4--dc23/eng/20240807
LC record available at https://lccn.loc.gov/2024028587
LC ebook record available at https://lccn.loc.gov/2024028588

Originally delivered by fleets of horse-drawn wagons, the affordable paperbacks from D. L. Moody's publishing house resourced the church and served everyday people. Now, after more than 125 years of publishing and ministry, Moody Publishers' mission remains the same—even if our delivery systems have changed a bit. For more information on other books (and resources) created from a biblical perspective, go to www.moodypublishers.com or write to:

Moody Publishers
820 N. LaSalle Boulevard
Chicago, IL 60610

1 3 5 7 9 10 8 6 4 2

Printed in the United States of America

This Light of Mine is dedicated to my beloved grandchildren and their spouses . . . Gabe and Allie, Olivia, Quinn and Callie, Bennett, Maggie, Cate, Sophie, Silas, Eli, and Lily . . . who will carry the light of Christ's kingdom into their worlds for the good of others and the glory of God. I am proud to be known as their "Papa"!

"Grandchildren are the crown of the aged" —Proverbs 17:6

CONTENTS

PREFACE

I have long wished that someone would address how followers of Jesus should respond to the dramatic shift in Western culture that we have experienced over the last few decades. We are good at identifying the ways our world has changed and good at being concerned about the impact of these changes. But we have not been as good about knowing what to do about it. We struggle with how to answer the question of the psalmist: "If the foundations are destroyed, what can the righteous do?" (Ps. 11:3).

While not being sure that I am the right one to be writing this book, I find myself concerned with the troubling effect of a lack of clear direction. This lack of direction impacts the primacy of the gospel, the supremacy of Jesus' kingdom, our allegiance to His ways, and the unity of His church. All these have been threatened by well-intended but less-than-helpful responses in attitudes and actions.

There is no doubt that any attempt at answering the question of what we should do in the face of the growing darkness in America is fraught with complex realities that are entwined in strong emotional, political, and relational dynamics. And while not all may agree with everything I have written, it is my hope that we can all agree that the gospel should be unhindered and that following the ways of Jesus into the darkness is the right approach. And I hope as well that together we can begin a conversation about what is good and necessary for us as followers of Jesus in terms of being able to impact our culture in a positive way for Christ and His kingdom.

It's my prayer that you will read this book with an open mind and join me in fulfilling Jesus' commission to empower the gospel in our dark world with the light of the kingdom of Christ!

It should be noted that I wrote *This Light of Mine* before the results of the 2024 US presidential election, in a season when many evangelicals felt a sense of hopelessness having lost the culture to a pagan agenda. As a result of the presidential election results, many evangelicals no longer feel quite so hopeless. The challenge now is that the election results might tempt us to place our ultimate hope in political victories that are temporary at best when God calls us to place our ultimate hope in Him and His faithfulness to us regardless of earthly circumstances.

While some may not feel like political losers given the election results, there are many cultural realities that this election will not change that still put evangelicals in the losing column of what is good and right for society. Most importantly, my desire in writing this book is to lead those of us who are followers of Jesus to be passionate about advancing the kingdom of Christ over any other earthly agenda, political or otherwise, and to live in the Jesus Way regardless of cultural wins and losses.

HOW SHOULD WE THEN LIVE?

·················

If the foundations are destroyed,
what can the righteous do?

PSALM 11:3

Soon after my retirement from Christian higher education, my wife, Martie, and I decided to take up a new way of life. Wanting to visit the national parks out west, we thought we'd get a camper and do it the right way. This was a high-risk adventure since we had never camped a day in our lives! Thankfully, we have come to love camping and living in faraway places off the beaten path.

As you may know, many campgrounds have shower facilities that provide the opportunity of freshening up while roughing it. One morning, on my way to the shower, I noticed a man in front of me with a towel rolled in his hand. I knew that he was headed to the shower and would probably beat me there. But he stopped at the sink to shave as I went on to claim one of the two shower stalls.

I greeted another guy who was preparing to step into the adjacent shower. He returned the greeting and began to tell me how terrible it was that in this day of "trans" rights and other items on the so-called progressive agenda, he wouldn't dare bring his young daughter to a shower at a campground. His monologue didn't stop there. While the two shower stalls were separate, the wall between us only went up about seven feet with an opening above. He went on about the horrible political and social climate in America and the power of the LGBTQ+ movement. Legalizing marijuana made his list of complaints. Gender identity pronouns and the lack of a definition of what a woman is also found a place in the diatribe. As the rant went on, individual politicians were also targeted. Then he said, "I go to a great church and my pastor is all over this stuff. He has no tolerance for any of it!"

When he said he went to church I thought, "Hey, he's a brother!" So, wanting to lower the temperature a bit, I said, "Yeah, but I've read the last chapter. King Jesus wins!"

He replied, "Right, but we've got to fight!"

He had every reason to be concerned. In fact, I share some of his concerns. But it was the hateful, fist-in-your face, warrior tone that bothered me. He and his pastor, like many politically annoyed parishioners and clergy today, had drawn a line in the sand and declared war: not just against the policies of the progressives but against the progressives themselves.

As I left the shower, the gentleman who had stopped to shave was waiting with his towel folded, next in line. There's no doubt that he had heard the rant. I felt embarrassed for the gospel. If someone would say to him, "Would you be interested in becoming a Christian? You could be just like us," it would be a nonstarter.

ATTITUDE SHIFT

Not all of us are angry. But there is a prevailing sense that we are the losers and that the bad guys have won, leaving us downhearted and fearful for the future. The problem with this kind of posture is that, given our privileged responsibility of attracting others to Jesus, no one is going to be attracted to a group of hopeless, despairing losers! People already have enough about which to despair. With rising rates of suicide, the crisis of anxiety among younger generations, chaos in our cities, random violence that terrorizes innocent people, and the prevailing anger and frustration with deepening divisions of racial and political issues, many in our world already feel a sense of hopelessness and despair.

I get the anger part. Every time I see a headline celebrating the advance of some progressive agenda that magnifies our loss, I feel the negative energy. And, I guess, there would be something wrong with me if I just shrugged it off as though it didn't make any difference.

CJ Stroud, rookie quarterback for the Houston Texans, is a deeply committed follower of Jesus. After defeating the Cleveland Browns

> *We need an attitude shift that puts out the welcome mat of the gospel to all.*

in the first round of the NFL playoff games, he started his after-game interview by saying, "First, I want to give all the glory to my Lord and Savior Jesus Christ!" I was watching the interview and was thrilled that a brother had turned the spotlight away from himself and onto Jesus. But when I noticed that NBC Sports, who put the interview on X, deleted his testimony, it triggered the kind of anger we feel when we are reminded of the disdain our world has for comments like that.[1] I thought, "Now they've canceled Jesus. So much for tolerance! Do I really live in an America where someone's testimony is banned from public discourse?"

So the issue is not the anger part. It's an internal trigger that something is wrong. The issue is knowing what to do with the negative energy that is triggered by the anger. Paul exhorts us, "Be angry and do not sin" (Eph. 4:26). That means that our anger—even when appropriate and righteous—can lead us to do the wrong kinds of things. Paul goes on to say, "Do not let the sun go down on your anger." So at best, our anger needs to be short-lived, without misguided actions, and channeled to positive outcomes.

We might dismiss the concerned shower-taker as a one-off. But being around Christians over the last couple of decades brings me to a different conclusion. The conclusion is that we need an attitude shift that presents an attractive alternative to a watching world and a clear strategy of biblically advised actions that puts out the welcome mat of the gospel to all.

IN THE TIMES WE ARE GIVEN

Francis Schaeffer asked in his now prophetic critique of the cultural shift, "How should we then live?"[2] Schaeffer and his wife, Edith, founded L'Abri ("shelter") in Switzerland in the 1970s, a place for seekers to talk and explore ideas about culture and spirituality. The Schaeffers' message was that Western society had changed because the foundation had shifted from a Christian basis to a secular one, from one based on eternal truths of God as Creator to one in which human beings are at the center. Sound familiar? And this was decades ago! It is no secret that the mores of our society have grown less God-centered since Dr. Schaeffer so presciently spoke.

American Christians are rightly concerned about the troubling realities of the shift in our culture. On nearly every front of society things are different now. And much of the shift is in direct contradiction to the convictions that we have cherished and consider to be divinely declared, leaving us with the sense that we have lost. There is a new sheriff in town, and it's not our kind of guy. Holding on to what in our eyes is good and right feels like a losing battle. In many ways, we have lost the role that Christianity played in promoting the Judeo-Christian values that governed life and defined our national identity. We feel like Frodo, in J. R. R. Tolkien's *The Fellowship of the Ring*, when he faced the danger of the Black Riders. "I knew that danger lay ahead, of course; but I did not expect to meet it in our own Shire."[3]

Some may be more optimistic than I am about getting America back on track and reclaiming the values that once united us. Yet it's hard to imagine that we could pivot to a cultural consensus about issues like the sanctity of life, human sexuality, gender, and changes to our definition of marriage. To again quote from Tolkien, Frodo says, "I wish none of this had happened." Wise Gandalf replies, "So do all who live to see such times, but that is not for them to decide. All we have to decide is what to do with the time that is given to us."[4]

"How should we then live?" remains a crucial question.

WHAT CAN THE RIGHTEOUS DO?

In one way, it's not difficult to answer the question. As Americans we have the advantage of influencing culture by supporting and voting for candidates that affirm and advance our values. We can attend meetings and run for school boards. We can take our place on county commissions. We can easily email our elected representatives and let them know how we as their constituents will vote. We might even run for public offices ourselves. We can volunteer to support the causes we feel are worthy of our time and effort. We can responsibly and courteously use social media to express our views. And, thankfully, pastors are still able to preach boldly into every aspect of life when it comes to clear biblical principles.

Though it rarely makes the news, followers of Christ and many churches and organizations are doing amazing things to influence our culture in a positive way.

But apart from these legitimate activities it is clear that many have opted for a variety of other approaches. Some are flat-out mad and in a fighting mood, placing their hope in political conquest. Others have acquiesced to the change and drifted downstream with the culture. Still others, in despair, have retreated into a holy huddle hoping that Jesus will soon return and rescue them . . . all of which are the wrong responses if we are evaluating the possibilities from a biblical perspective.

By *not* knowing what the right thing is to do, I fear we may actually be doing the wrong things in response to the shift. Like children who want to help Dad with a project and who, in spite of their good intentions, actually get in the way and do more harm than good.

This is not to say we're all doing more harm than good. Though it rarely makes the news, followers of Christ and many churches and organizations are doing amazing things to influence our culture in positive ways—ways that are in sync with what Jesus would do, and ways we can be lights in the darkness.

But some have done more harm than good by moving into our culture with angry attitudes and misguided actions, and evangelical Christians are often called out on this point. Not every Christian is an evangelical, of course, but I'm assuming that most of you reading this book identify as such. Unfortunately, evangelicals are often better known for political positions than allegiance to Christ and His kingdom. Sadly, often the marriage of our faith with politics is accompanied by hostile, warring attitudes toward others who don't share our values.

It should be noted here that "evangelical" is not always easily defined. But while it is difficult to nail down every aspect of evangelicalism, British historian David Bebbington has articulated the following four widely accepted identifiers of an evangelical.[5]

- Biblicism: the high view of the authority of Scripture
- Crucicentrism: the centrality of the work of the cross and its saving benefit

- Conversionism: the desire to convert others to the saving work of Jesus
- Activism: sharing the message of the gospel through tangible actions

While all evangelicals are Christians, not all Christians would consider themselves to be evangelical. And though the general feeling among many is that evangelicals are aligned with a right-wing political ideology, not all evangelicals would identify with that assessment.

WHAT IS JESUS' WAY?

In light of this often-negative approach toward those who don't share our values and our propensity to politicize our faith, this would be a good time to ask, "What would Jesus want us to do?" Thankfully, He has a better way. A way that transforms our attitudes and redirects our actions to positive outcomes in terms of influencing our culture and drawing curious observers to Himself.

So before we ask with the psalmist, "What can the righteous do when the foundations are destroyed?" (Ps. 11:13), let's look to Jesus. If we are willing to ask what He would have us do, we must brace ourselves for some revolutionary answers that contradict our normal instincts. When it comes to engaging culture, Jesus has a far different agenda that is in sync with a far different kingdom than the kingdoms of this world. Remember the Lord's words to Isaiah? He reminded him that His thoughts and His ways are different than those of mankind (Isa. 55:8). So I'll warn you: the agenda is challenging. It's an agenda that is counterintuitive and easy to dismiss if you're looking for a strategy that seems instinctively right to you.

When it comes to influencing our culture for Christ, His ways will seem too soft to some. Too slow to turn the tables on our world for others. Too much like a skewed or watered-down gospel to a few. Too much like a losing strategy to those who think we need to fight if we are to win. If we are given to our natural instincts, it will be easy to resist His ways and proceed with what *we* think may be right.

In the end, it doesn't make much difference what I write in terms of influencing our fallen culture for Christ. If it's just what I think, then its validity is up for grabs. But if it's clearly what Jesus has prescribed, then the argument is with Him: the one who is *the* way and *the* truth.

TO THINK ABOUT

How would you describe your attitude toward the shift in our culture?
Would you be willing to surrender to the ways of Jesus regardless
of what they might be?

TWO

THY KINGDOM COME

....

"But who do you say that I am?"

MATTHEW 16:15

When we bemoan the growing godlessness of our culture, we must remember that Jesus was born into an environment governed by a pagan Roman empire whose permissive behavior would make a modern heathen blush. It was an oppressive political culture that held Israel under its totalitarian thumb. The average Jew of that day would feel like they had lost, and that the glory days of Israel were long past. They longed for the arrival of the liberating Messiah whom the prophets had promised. And Jesus claimed to be their man!

Yet, what was troubling about Him was that He wasn't in sync with their expectations. He was a surprise. His leading passion was to do His Father's will, which clearly did not include the overthrow of the political and cultural demons of His day. Instead, He focused His attention on calling out a cohort of those who would follow Him into the lives of the poor, the marginalized, the sick, and the outcast with the good news of a far better kingdom to come. We must not miss that His harshest words were not for the powers of Rome but on the pride of hypocritical religious leaders and chief priests who had compromised themselves with allegiances to the political systems of their day. Uninterested in courting those in the halls of power or in seeking to leverage the political systems, He walked into the lives of sinners, like tax collectors or a "woman of the city" (Luke 7:37). He even engaged with the "unclean": ceremonially unclean people like lepers, women with issues of blood, and demoniacs were the targets of His energy and love.

By His actions and words, He was defining who He was and His purpose, which was different from what they had expected. Even John the Baptist had a question he asked his disciples to convey to Jesus: "Are you the one who is to come, or shall we look for another?" Jesus rolled out His messianic credentials by saying, "Go and tell John what you have seen and heard: the blind receive their sight, the lame walk, lepers are cleansed, and the deaf hear, the dead are raised up, the poor have good news preached to them" (Luke 7:19–22).

The shocking thing about Jesus and His ministry is that instead of castigating the sinners who were reviled and rejected by religious people as cultural enemies, He hung out with them.

The establishment was scandalized when He told a story about the value of a prodigal son (Luke 15:11–32). In another parable, the hero was a political enemy, as Jesus used a Samaritan to answer the question of who our neighbors are (Luke 10:25–37). At risk to His reputation back in Jerusalem, He conversed at a well with a woman who was also from the enemy territory of Samaria, to offer her the redeeming love of the living water (John 4:1–42).

Add to that, He healed a Roman centurion's servant and celebrated the centurion's faith as being greater than the faith of those in Israel (Luke 7:1–10). He also pursued a dinner invitation with the most reviled person in town, a tax collector, who had climbed a tree to see Him (Luke 19:1–10). Clarifying why He wanted to go to Zacchaeus' house, He said, "The Son of Man came to seek and save the lost" (v 10).

WHO IS JESUS?

If someone were to ask you, "Who do you say Jesus is?" what would you say? Creator? Savior? Friend? All great answers but of little help in terms of our responding effectively in an increasingly hostile environment. If, however, you would have said, "Joe, thanks for asking! He is my conquering King!" you would be on the road to transforming your attitudes. You're not a loser if your King is the conqueror and you're not intimidated by earthly powers since He has done all that is necessary to ultimately defeat evil.

Jesus took His disciples to a hostile and intimidating place and asked them the same question: Who do you think I am? The location where He asked this question and the answer He was looking for are instructive.

In an effort to mitigate the disciples' "loser" mentality, Jesus took them on a tour of one of the most decadent places in Palestine, Caesarea Philippi. Caesarea Philippi was a Roman colony north of the Sea of Galilee. It had a notable temple to the emperor and was also the global headquarters of the worship of the god Pan. No Jew worthy of his Torah would be caught near its red-light district. To Jews, emperor worship was a direct affront to their allegiance to the one true God. And the festivals in honor of Pan were openly shameful events that included bestiality and way-out-of-bounds wickedness. It was here, in the heart of heretical and debauched paganism, that He asked the disciples the leading question, "Who do people say that the Son of Man is?" They answered, "Some say John the Baptist, others say Elijah, and others Jeremiah or one of the prophets."

Then He said to them, "But who do *you* say that I am?" And Peter jumped in with his answer: "You are the Christ, the Son of the living

> He said to them, "But who do you say that I am?" And Peter jumped in with his answer: "You are the Christ, the Son of the living God." Jesus affirmed this truth.

God." Jesus affirmed this truth and responded that Peter's answer came from the "Father who is in heaven" (Matt. 16:13–17).

When Peter said "you are the Christ," he was using the Hebrew word for Messiah. Peter was affirming that Jesus was the long-awaited promise of the prophets. And to add to that, Peter personally believed that Jesus was, as he said, the "Son of the living God." This statement was a recognition that in a world of gods of wood and stone that couldn't hear or help—right in the territory of worship to the god Pan and the worship to the emperor—Jesus was the Son of the one and only true God who was alive and capable of blessing and benefitting all who would come to Him.

In fact, Jesus continued bolstering the sense of the disciples' confidence and courage with the winning promise that He would build His church and that "the gates of hell" would not prevail against it.

What Peter Misunderstood

Peter gets an A+ in theology!

But the star student isn't at the head of the class for long. Matthew in his gospel went on to say that Jesus began to explain to His disciples that He was going to Jerusalem where He would "suffer many things . . . and be killed" (Matt.16:21). Hearing this, Peter pulls Jesus aside and said, "Far be it from you, Lord! This shall *never* happen to you" (v. 22). While Peter had the right answer to Jesus' messianic identity and divine nature, it is clear he was still locked into the mistaken notion that the mission of the coming Messiah would be to overthrow the pagan Roman rule and restore Israel to its former glory, and sit on the throne of David to rule in righteousness and justice. Any thought of Jesus, the Messiah, going to the cross was a direct and disappointing contradiction of this widely held expectation. And it would have been anathema to Peter, and others, who expected a messianic victory over the political and social evils of his day.

Though Peter gets an A+ in theology, he got an F in politics, given his zeal for the restoration of an earthly kingdom.

Interestingly, Jesus reproved Peter in the strongest of terms. He says, "Get behind me, Satan! You are a hindrance to me. For you are not setting your mind on the things of God, but on the things of man" (Matt. 16:23). God evidently had a different messianic plan than those whose minds were on the overthrow of earthly kingdoms.

The reference to Satan is a flashback to Christ's temptation in the wilderness at the beginning of His ministry. That's when Satan offered Jesus all the kingdoms of this world and their glory if He would simply bow down and worship Satan (Matt. 4:9–10). But Jesus knew that as the true Messiah, He was not to become the ruler of kingdoms of this world, as enticing as that may seem, but to bring another, far more significant kingdom that would ultimately conquer the kingdoms of this world (1 Cor. 15:24–28). It would be a heavenly kingdom whose victory would be sealed by the defeat of the real enemy, Satan. A kingdom that would be launched by Jesus here on earth and consummated in its wonderful fullness in eternity. Forever!

Peter's ear-cutting episode in the garden of Gethsemane seems to indicate that in spite of Jesus' repeated teaching on the arrival of His kingdom, Peter remained focused on fighting for an earthbound kingdom. He reminds me of the shower-taker who said, "Right, but we've got to fight!"

Interestingly, the resurrection pivoted Peter from being an earthly militant to becoming a passionate advocate for the kingdom of Christ. He takes the pulpit at Pentecost and three thousand people join the kingdom as the church is born. And, at the end of his distinguished life as a leading light in the early church, he was crucified in Rome as a martyr. In honor of Jesus, he requested to be crucified upside down because he felt that he was not worthy to die as Jesus did.

Caravaggio's dramatic painting of Peter's crucifixion hangs in the Cerasi Chapel of the Church of Santa Maria del Popolo in Rome. The painting is positioned next to the altar of the chapel. In his work, Caravaggio painted Peter looking toward the altar instead of looking at the soldiers who were tying him to his cross, depicting that Peter lived and died with confidence in the victorious work of Christ on his behalf. It is clear that even in death, he never thought of himself as a loser.

BRIDGES? OR BARRIERS?

I fear that our legitimate concern for the cultural drift of American society has recruited many to prioritize the rescue of our earthly kingdom in a way that has put the advance of His kingdom at risk.

In a Barna survey conducted in 2019 of how non-Christians view evangelicals, it is clear that our political posture is a predominant identifier of our movement. While the survey was taken a few years ago, as I write this reading the headlines and listening to political commentary, there is no doubt that this issue remains in force today—if not more so. The survey analysis notes, "As the U.S. enters another heated election year, a new Barna report shows Americans seem to increasingly view evangelicals through a political lens, which corresponds with mixed feelings toward this religious group."[6]

It's those "mixed feelings" that should trouble us. If people have "mixed feelings" toward us because of our stand for the righteous ways of Christ, no problem. But if they have "mixed feelings" because of our political posturing, as the survey reveals, we have created an offense to the gospel that has eclipsed its primacy and power. This is a problem.

In the article summarizing the findings of the survey, "US Adults See Evangelicals Through a Political Lens," the Barna Group states,

> Of course, it's most important that Christians of all traditions, evangelical or otherwise, concern themselves with the reputation of Jesus, not merely the perceptions of evangelicals. Yet, will the public witness of evangelicals be a bridge or a barrier to the very thing they hold most dear: persuading others to put their faith in Christ? The findings strongly suggest that the perceptions of evangelicals are more of a barrier than bridge on the road to gaining a hearing for the gospel. The results of this research requires soul searching among Christians. We need to discern a way forward with the current "evangelical brand."[7]

Reading Barna's survey reminded me of a conversation that I had with a friend. "You're an evangelical, right?" she asked. I answered yes, but immediately thought of the perceptions that she probably had about evangelicals and political alignments. The conversation quickly moved in another direction, but I wished I had had more time to nuance my response.

So how did we get to the place where we are seen as a political movement, or "seen through a political lens"? And is it possible that this approach has been "more of a barrier than bridge" to the effectiveness of the gospel?

While Martie and I were driving through the Louisiana countryside, we passed a beautiful ranch with white fences and horses grazing in the pastures. Along the fence by the road were several flags waving in the breeze promoting the residents' choice for president. When we reached the entrance drive, there was a prominent banner that read in large letters

JESUS, and in smaller print below His name, OUR ONLY HOPE. It's our right, as citizens of a free country, to put up Christian banners and political flags. But as I drove past the house, it was evident that the two were in tandem, and I wondered whether this person's Christian witness was helped or hurt by combining the messages.

There is nothing wrong with preferring one political party over another, or of identifying as right or left. But when we platform our preferred political candidates at national gatherings of evangelicals, or if high profile evangelical leaders publicly endorse preferred candidates, or when pastors host candidates in their pulpits, it gives the impression that we are a political force. Opening political rallies with partisan prayers and singing worship songs at the outset of gatherings focused on political campaigns has caused observers to conclude that conservative politics and evangelicalism are bedfellows. I wonder sometimes if our evangelical endorsements may leave some questioning if, in joining the kingdom, they have to become right-wing patriots to close the deal. And churches that position themselves politically face the danger of being known not for their gospel message but rather for their political identity.

. . . .

The events of January 6, 2021, were several years ago, and yet for many Americans, the sight of rioters at the Capitol remains seared in our memories. It was shocking to see many of those at the January 6 rally in DC brandishing signs that identified Jesus with their cause, while ugly words spouted from the mouths of those who purported to be devoted to Him—or at least identified Him with their cause.

In the midst of the political heat over immigration policy, a bus tour called the Army of God traveled to the Texas border and held rallies promoting its anti-immigrant point of view. And, according to news reports, members of the tour harassed the immigrants, with one Army of God participant telling reporters that he was used to hunting for animals but this was the first time he was hunting for people.[8] I'm not sure what God thinks of borders and immigration policy, but I do know that to portray ourselves as God's army coming to fight for a particular political preference is a rather bold step in the wrong direction.

As I watched the 2024 World Series, I noticed that commercial advertisements had been sewn onto the uniforms of many of the players. This means that our sports heroes are not only carrying the brand of their team but also the brand of someone else's products. When the world sees Jesus in us, they should see the life-giving brand of His gospel and that alone. He wears no other brand! Attaching political identities to His brand is not only a terrible distraction but, as Barna notes, a barrier to the gospel for many who see us as an opposing political force rather than a life-giving resource.

In our passion to rescue America, it's been easy for some to place their ultimate hope in electing a political savior at any cost. Let's say that our efforts resulted in a political victory, a victory that in the short run would be commendable. Yet such a victory would be at best temporary. If we were to gain a political victory at the expense of drawing a lost world to the Savior, the damage would be more significant than the victory. Add to that the compromising of our own values to do whatever is necessary to win our culture back to our way of thinking.

Righting a Misguided Approach

There are some who tell us that we need to make every effort to get America "back," because, they believe, America is a covenant nation that has been singled out by God for blessing and favor; that we are the new Israel. In light of that, we have a divine duty to win it back for Him and His glory, and that political conquest is the means to the divinely intended end.

The problem with this perspective is that there is no biblical justification for this kind of Christian nationalistic thinking. And, if we believe it is God's favored nation and it's our job to reclaim it, we risk embarrassing Him if it doesn't get reclaimed. And now, not only are we the losers, but it makes it appear that God is the loser as well.

Granted, America was founded by those who believed that God and His laws were fundamental to a flourishing society and that for nearly two centuries, generally speaking, America embraced a national consensus that the Judeo-Christian laws of God were good and right. But our prosperity and favor were not a result of God selecting us to be His favored nation but rather due to the fact that no matter who you are or where you live, living in the lane of God's ways contributes to a flourishing life and society. Like trees planted by rivers of water eloquently described in Psalm 1, those who delight in the law of God prosper.

Some forms of Christian nationalism advance the belief that the role of government is to guarantee that America is a Christian nation. And that places of power should be held only by Christians who enforce the laws of Christianity. In this context, those who are not Christians are seen as second-class citizens. Some proponents of this way of thinking go so far as believing a citizen should be a Christian in order to be "truly American."

When a Muslim family moved in next door, my friend wanted to find a way to interest them in Jesus. That sure beats the "there goes the neighborhood" attitude that many would have had.

I wonder if it ever occurred to us that America is now a multicultural nation and that many of our neighbors and coworkers are not Christian Americans. After generations of sending missionaries around the world, God has now sent the mission field to live in our towns and neighborhoods. For many, our mission field now lives next door. Do we really think that the gospel will be an attractive alternative for those who feel we have relegated them to second-class citizenship?

When I was pastoring in the Detroit area, one of the men from our congregation asked me if I knew of any reading that he could get on how to lead Muslims to Christ. I asked him why he was interested. He told me that a Muslim family had moved in next door and that he wanted to find a way to interest them in Jesus. That sure beats the "there goes the neighborhood" attitude that many would have had.

There is a growing movement that feels like the drastic issues of our day need a drastic response. They postulate that our former strategies for influencing the culture are no longer effective given the radical shift in our society and its increasing hostility to our convictions.

I find this concerning. We should be suspicious of any plan that supplants the ways of Jesus. The thought that we need to shift tactics because of the drastic times in which we live ignores an important fact—Jesus articulated His plan in a time when followers faced a far more hostile environment than the situation we face today. Into a world of debauched paganism and the inevitable persecution of believers, He said, "Blessed are you when others revile you and persecute you and utter all kinds of evil against you falsely on my account" (Matt. 5:11). He then followed with instructions on how to respond, saying,

> "You are the light of the world. A city set on a hill cannot be hidden. Nor do people light a lamp and put it under a basket, but on a stand, and it gives light to the whole house. In the same way, let your light shine before others, so that they may see your good works and give glory to your Father who is in heaven." (vv. 14–16)

Interestingly, Peter repeats the strategy to early Christians who faced violent opposition by saying, "Keep your conduct among the Gentiles honorable, so that when they speak against you as evildoers,

they may see your good deeds and glorify God on the day of visitation"
(1 Peter 2:12).

LIGHT THE DARKNESS

Jesus' plan is clear. We are to light up the darkness with the light of our
good works. And while this may seem rather naïve to some as an effective
strategy, as we will see later in the book, the early Christians practiced this
effectively and with God-glorifying outcomes. And this is the case for the
many churches, individuals, and organizations in our day who are living
out Christ's plan and offering to their communities an attractive alternative to the emptiness of life without God. I know of no other strategy in
Scripture than the way of Jesus. Nor is there any notion that His strategy
has expired. More on this later.

As we have said, one thing is clear. Our political alignments do, in
effect, as Barna notes, build a barrier rather than a bridge to a significant
portion of our population that no longer thinks of evangelicals as Christ
followers but as a political force that they oppose. I think you would
agree that exchanging the rightful place of Jesus as the centerpiece for a
reputation of political identity is not a good exchange. Especially when
reaching our whole community for Christ is our priority.

Doing It Right

Chris Goeppner pastors a flourishing church in the shadow of Dartmouth College, a leading Ivy League university. One would think that
it would be a tough place to do church given the political environment,
in which the progressive agenda is flourishing. But Chris sees people
coming to the Lord on a regular basis, and this growing church is well
thought of in the community. Not because they have hidden their commitment to biblical truth and morality or compromised their stand.
Quite the opposite. Chris stands firm on the essentials. Instead, their

church is known for sharing the love of Christ with the needs of the region, which clearly has opened the hearts of the townspeople to the church's message of the hope and restoration that only Jesus can give.

This church is known for sharing the love of Christ with the needs of the region. No wonder they see people responding to their message of hope in Christ!

Among other things, the church consistently feeds public school teachers lunch; they have paid off the school lunch debts of hundreds of students; they provide volunteers for community recreational activities in nearby towns; they provide monthly volunteer support for a destitute town's soup kitchen, and their Care Ministry has helped with hundreds of families' heating bills and repairs in the harsh New England winters. It's no wonder they see people responding to their message of hope in Christ!

I've often thought that if Chris had decided to take up war against the progressive agenda in his area and to politicize his ministry, his opportunity to keep the gospel appealing would have been wasted. Thankfully, his church has sought to advance Christ's kingdom by blessing those who some would feel are our enemies and by serving the welfare of their community. And it can't go unnoticed that what this church is doing is directly in line with Jesus' words to His people who lived in a hostile culture when He said that they were to be lights in the darkness. Lights that conquer the darkness by good works. Works that bless others (Matt. 5:11–16)!

Other lights shine amid tough surroundings. Ailyn says, "During my time at Dartmouth, God opened doors in ways I never imagined. I came into college having freshly decided I wanted to follow Jesus again. God led me to connect with Cru, a campus ministry whose members encouraged me to pursue Him for

> myself. To me, Cru was evidence that even in the midst of an environment that often dismisses Christian values, God was faithful in providing me the light that led me to His heart." Keli adds, "Being part of the Christian community at a secular university was the pinnacle of my college experience. Through the faith of my mentors and peers, I was able to see God moving on a campus that tries to push God to the background. Witnessing God's work in the lives of others and experiencing His presence in our gatherings brought so much light and love to my time at college."

"The Welfare of the City"

As we have noted, the singular mission of Jesus was to initiate and advance the kingdom of His Father. When teaching His disciples, He instructed them to pray, "Your kingdom come, your will be done, on earth as it is in heaven" (Matt. 6:10). We know His will is already being done in heaven. His kingdom, which we need to advance on earth, is one whose reign over the hearts of humankind is both spiritual and eternal with significant cultural benefit to all who would enter it and live by its distinctives. His kingdom brings solutions that heal and dissolve the divisiveness, hate, and chaos of earthly rivalries.

As we advance His kingdom, we are reminded that Scripture calls us to share this kingdom with our fellow countrymen.

This is why Jesus, in His Sermon on the Mount, which in a sense is like the constitution of His kingdom, told His followers to turn the other cheek and to love their enemy, a standard that made for peace and not war. When we as His kingdom citizens bring the dynamics of His kingdom to bear upon the kingdoms of this fallen world, regardless of the cost, there is the potential for significant influence for good and God's glory.

Too often we have cared more about our earthly kingdom than we have cared about His heavenly kingdom here on earth. And to reclaim our earthly kingdom, we have too often hidden the door to Christ's eternal kingdom—a kingdom that is above all kingdoms. A kingdom that we have been called to advance for His name and for His glory (1 Peter 2:9; Rev. 1:6).

As we advance His kingdom, we are reminded that Scripture calls us to share this kingdom with our fellow countrymen. And this is regardless of their political preferences or personal positions on issues with which we disagree. Again, Jesus' call on our lives is to take the gospel into *all* the world, into a world that is fundamentally unfriendly to us.

None of this is to say that He didn't care about the fallen culture of His day or the importance of influencing it for good. He did, and He cares about ours. It's just that He had a different strategy: a strategy that revolved around the dictates of a different kind of King and a different kind of kingdom—and it's a strategy that infuses our losing attitudes with confidence and courage in light of the victorious, conquering reign of this King. For all of us who are intimidated by the powers that reign on earth and for all of us who feel hopeless and despairing as though we are the losers, embracing the ramifications of this other-kingdom strategy is an important step toward living well in a world gone wrong.

> None of this is to say that He didn't care about the fallen culture of His day or the importance of influencing it for good.

Granted, if the darkness resists us because of our stand on clear biblical definitions of right and wrong, we will join the masses who throughout church history have stood regardless of the cost. But if they stop listening to us because we have staged them as our enemy or they find our attitudes unappealing or see us as a fringe subculture on the political landscape that they want nothing to do with, we have failed in our responsibility to welcome all into His kingdom. As Tim Keller rightly reminded us, "Though the gospel is unavoidably offensive, we must work hard to make sure people are offended by the gospel itself rather than our personal, cultural, and political derivations."[9] It's inconceivable to think that entering into warfare with those who oppose us will cultivate the ground for them to want to know about our Jesus. We can't have it both ways, which amplifies how important it is to respond in Jesus' way.

When the Jews were in captivity in Babylon, rather than calling them to fight for their rights or encouraging them to subversively overthrow the evil regime, Jeremiah writes to them,

> Thus says the LORD of hosts, the God of Israel, to all exiles whom I have sent into exile from Jerusalem to Babylon: Build houses and live in them; plant gardens and eat their produce . . . seek the welfare of the city where I have sent you into exile and pray to the LORD on its behalf, for in its welfare you will find your welfare. (Jer. 29:4–5, 7)

The Assignment

When Jesus began His ministry tour, after recruiting Peter, Andrew, James, and John (Matt. 4:18–22), He didn't head for Jerusalem, where He could network with political power brokers and marketing experts who could set the stage for messianic conquest. Rather, as Matthew notes, "he went throughout all Galilee . . . proclaiming the gospel of the kingdom and healing every disease and every affliction among the people" (4:23). The kingdom of heaven on earth is a constant theme for Christ. He tells parables to explain the dynamics of His kingdom, and He heals the sick to demonstrate that in His kingdom there is ultimately no sickness or sorrow. It's like a sneak preview to the really big show to come (Rev. 21:4). Remember that when Pilate asked Him if He was the king of the Jews, Jesus replied, "My kingdom is not of this world. If my kingdom were of this world my servants would have been fighting, that I might not be delivered over to the Jews. But my kingdom is not of this world" (John 18:36).

If regaining our earthly kingdom distracts us in the advance of His kingdom, we have failed in our allegiance to Christ's call in our lives.

Initiating and advancing the reign and rule of His kingdom was not only Jesus' mission but the assignment that He gave to the disciples. And, more importantly for our discussion, we by God's awesome grace and love have been placed into the kingdom of Christ, and advancing it is our calling as well. And while it is easy to be distracted with the compelling thought that our pressing priority is to reclaim our earthly kingdom, if regaining our earthly kingdom distracts or diminishes our potential for success in the advance of His kingdom, we have failed in our allegiance to Christ's call in our lives. Embracing the supremacy of our kingdom calling over all earthly concerns makes all the difference in terms of adjusting our feelings and actions in response to a culture that is so desperately out of sync with His kingdom.

─────── **TO THINK ABOUT** ───────

Do you find that you have more passion for reforming earthly kingdoms than you do for advancing the kingdom of Christ? What would look different in your attitudes and actions in response to the cultural shift if you were driven to make Christ and the ways of His kingdom known?

THREE

CONFIDENCE, COURAGE, AND COMPASSION

. . . .

In all these things we are more than conquerors.

ROMANS 8:37

Christians in the early centuries of the church were in trouble because they were trouble—trouble to the pagan systems of their day. They were in trouble because of what they believed and what they taught and how they lived. Their beliefs were not just different from widely held cultural ideals, but the truths that they held dear were a threat to the accepted norms of their day.

TROUBLING THE WORLD

Christians were viewed as a threat to the theological systems of their day. The new faith started as a sect of Judaism, and its adherents met and worshiped in the synagogues. But their proclamation that Jesus was the true Messiah who had risen from the dead was ultimately too much for the Jewish leaders. So they were thrown out of the synagogues and forced to meet in homes.

Christians were perceived as an economic threat. Some early Christians lost their jobs because they refused to pay homage to the god of their guild. In the minds of the pagans, this would anger the god of their guild and depreciate the success of the business.

Christians were a threat to the religious aspirations of the Roman culture. Early followers believed that there was only one God and that all other gods were idolatrous and false. In a world that held that there was a multiplicity of gods who could be cajoled to satisfy the desires of the populace, the thought that their gods were illegitimate was blasphemous and unacceptable.

Christians were a threat to the political priorities of their day. Emperor worship was the glue that held the empire together. Often at festivals and official gatherings, the loyalty of the crowds was expressed by the boisterous chant, "Caesar is Lord!" Followers of Jesus couldn't join the chorus because Jesus was their Lord. This made them a political threat, and many paid the price for their assumed insurrectionist intentions by going face-to-face with wild animals.

Christians were a threat to the prejudiced, privileged social structures of their day. The caste system of Roman society was a valued way of advantaging rich and highly positioned individuals. Early Christians met in their homes and welcomed all to join them. Slaves, freemen, the disabled, wealthy aristocrats, women, Jews, Gentiles . . . all were equally valued and warmly welcomed. I can imagine the shock as wide-eyed neighbors watched believers gathering at the house across the street given the diversity of congregation.

Christians were a threat to family values. Family was a highly valued social structure in Roman culture. Interestingly enough, the core of family was not the parents but the siblings, the brothers and sisters. Early Christians called each other "brother" and "sister" and were thus perceived as hijacking the importance of true brothers and sisters.

Christians were a threat to the cultural perceptions of wealth and status. In Roman society, having servants and slaves was a badge of prosperity and honor. It must have seemed strange to the average person that Christians counted it a privilege to serve each other, to serve their neighbor, and specifically to serve the poor. Interestingly, this commitment to serving others became a power move in Christians' efforts to influence their culture for Christ. More on this in chapters to come.

Needless to say, nearly every aspect of a Christian's life under Roman rule was impacted with the pressures of being countercultural.

You'd think that with all these pressures on their lives, Christians in the first centuries would have bailed on what they believed to lessen the pain. Or worse yet, been unfaithful to the truths of Jesus as taught by the apostles to be more acceptable in society. After all, who wants to be socially and economically ostracized and politically out of touch?

Admirably, they stayed the course! Truth was not a dispensable commodity and faithfulness to their Lord was the highest priority.

CONFIDENCE AND COURAGE . . . IN THE MIDST OF CULTURAL PRESSURE

Two virtues that kept our ancestors in the faith strong in the midst of pressure were confidence and courage. They were confident that Jesus was indeed the "truth." Though the world pointed an accusing finger at them, they had the unwavering confidence that Jesus and His ways were right and that His truth as taught by Him and the apostles did not have an expiration date. And their courage was bolstered by Jesus' words, "Blessed are those who are persecuted for righteousness' sake, for theirs is the kingdom of heaven. Blessed are you when others revile you and persecute you and utter all kinds of evil against you falsely on my account. Rejoice and be glad, for your reward is great in heaven" (Matt. 5:10–12). Note that the persecution of Christians came because they practiced the righteous ways of Jesus and were suffering for the sake of Christ's name, not because they were annoying people with unattractive attitudes.

The difficulty with early Christians was that they were different, a difference that was a threat to the world they lived in. But their difference should not be a surprise. They were people of a different kingdom, a kingdom with different rules and ways than those of Rome.

Inevitable Tension

The challenge for us is the same. If we are in sync with the ways of Christ's kingdom, we are different. And this difference is a threat to the values that our culture embraces . . . the values it considers to be good and right.

We need to realize that people with a politically progressive bent don't wake up in the morning thinking, *Aha! Another day to infuse evil into society.* They are convinced that what they believe and promote is best for our world. They envision a bright new day in America where all are free to live without restraint. They are committed to a new agenda with new ways of thinking and living. For them humankind is at the center of the universe. They hold to a worldview in which there are no absolutes, no restrictive moral authority, and where there is no "true truth" but where "your truth and my truth" are celebrated. So from their perspective, what we as Christians believe and teach gets in the way of their progress. Hence the pressure against people like you and me and why canceling us and our values is so important to them.

> *Two issues in particular seems to kick up the most dust for Christians in terms of cultural alienation.*

So again, we need to ask, "How should we then live?"

The issue for us is whether or not we will stand for truth with courage and confidence regardless of the outcomes as our brothers and sisters did in those early days of Christianity. And just as important, whether or not we will reject a militant warrior attitude and take our stand with attitudes that reflect the love of Christ. While finding ways to love those who perceive us as enemies is not always easy (Matt. 5:43), it is not hard to say what is not loving in terms of attitude and action toward those who disdain us.

The list of the tension points between our beliefs and the prevailing mores of our culture is long, but some issues seem to kick up the most dust for Christians in terms of cultural alienation. Two in particular: human sexuality and the sanctity of life.

I realize that mentioning these two raises the concern of those who accuse us of being a two-issue movement. We are often accused of ignoring other important issues like racial justice, poverty, creation care, the global refugee crisis, and other important cultural challenges that need addressing. And while, quite frankly, we could be doing better to engage our world with loving actions on those fronts, the charge that we are ignoring those cultural needs is not well founded.

Many within evangelicalism have raised their voices about the need for racial justice. Sadly, this comes often in the face of internal opposition from those who have been influenced by non-biblical perspectives on race. Local issues of poverty are being creatively addressed by many churches and evangelical organizations. Given that God's initial work order for those made in His image was to have dominion over all creation, there are some who are outspokenly addressing the need for creation care. And churches, mission organizations, and many Christ-following individuals are finding successful ways to minister to the needs of migrants and refugees.

But I mention the two issues above because they, more than any others, are the source of mounting, intimidating pressure against us, testing our resolve to confidently and courageously stand in sync with the principles of His kingdom as expressed in God's Word.

HUMAN SEXUALITY

The LBGTQ+ agenda is an intense source of pressure for many evangelicals. Standing for a biblical position on human sexuality is not just out of step but radically off the charts of decency for most secular people. The gay rights movement labels us as haters who want to rob people of the chance to live out their preferred sexual identity, so we are shamed, perceived as bigots, fill-in-the-blank-phobes, and deniers of the exercise of personal freedom. Granted, some of our poor attitudes toward same-sex-attracted people and others under the LBGTQ+ umbrella may deserve the criticism. But the pressure to go soft on what is clearly biblical is immense.

A friend of our family worked as a banker for a well-known national bank. He was highly successful and had a lengthy contact list of repeat customers he serviced. As a committed follower of Jesus, a serious issue arose when the company put out a call asking employees to attend the local gay pride parade and carry signs expressing the bank's support. Employees who signed up had their pictures posted on the company website and were celebrated for complying with the request.

Knowing that in good conscience he couldn't attend, our friend had several conversations with his colleagues about why he couldn't participate, explaining his faith in what Scripture taught about human sexuality and marriage. In his words, "It was not received well, to put it mildly."

He called the CEO at national headquarters to appeal, asking if the bank could also support those who had different convictions about the issue. In response, the CEO told him if he couldn't agree with the company's agenda, he should look for another job. If staying meant that he agreed with the company's agenda, as the CEO said, he knew that he couldn't stay. After discussing the ramifications with his wife, they agreed that he should not continue to work at the bank in violation of his conscience, and he resigned. His decision reflected his confidence and courage in the truth and values of the kingdom of Christ regardless of outward circumstances and outcomes. It reminded me of those early Christians who could not in good conscience worship the idols of the guild. My friend is now serving with an outstanding local ministry and told me, "I am so thankful!"

When I was serving as president of Cornerstone University, laws were being presented to Congress that were designed to cut off any federal funds to schools that didn't hire faculty and staff who were openly and actively gay. Had those legislative efforts passed we would have lost $25 million a year in government loans to our students. This would have been a financial loss that would be impossible for us to recover. It would have been game over if we didn't comply with the requirement. While we wouldn't have conceded to the pressure, I understand that the temptation for educational institutions to fold under the pressure is intense.

> *In the midst of pressure, many have had confidence in the truth regarding sexuality as taught in Scripture and had the courage to stay the course.*

The venomous marginalization that comes from cultural disdain is so immense that many mainline denominations decided to join the cultural majority by ordaining gay clergy and supporting same-sex marriage. There is a growing movement under the banner of "progressive" Christianity that affirms the cultural consensus on issues of human sexuality and same-sex marriage, and some churches, colleges, and ministries have joined them in bending the knee to the cultural shift. It seems interesting to me that the church at large for two thousand years has supported the view that Scripture is clear both exegetically and hermeneutically regarding our sexuality and the principle of marriage. Yet, when the culture shifts and castigates us for not going with them, we suddenly see the issues from a different point of view.

However, in the midst of pressure, others have had confidence in the truth regarding sexuality as taught in Scripture and had the courage to stay the course. There have been groups from Presbyterian, Methodist, Reformed, and other mainline denominations that are committed to upholding the biblical position on human sexuality that have separated and started their own fellowships. Anglicans in particular have been through challenging times over ordination of gay clergy and approval of same-sex marriage. Interestingly, the vast majority of Anglican bishops in Africa have stood firm in opposition to the ordination of gay clergy and the "blessing" of same-sex couples. Bishops in Africa made this statement, "Since the Lord does not bless same-sex unions, it is pastorally deceptive and blasphemous to craft prayers that invoke blessing in the name of the Father, Son, and Holy Spirit." In fact, their opposition to this cultural drift has delayed the Anglican Church from moving forward in its concession to the cultural pressure.

Tough Calls

One of the most difficult issues we face in responding well to LGBTQ+ issues is when a loved one is proposing to move ahead with a relationship or marriage that's out of sync with the will and ways of God. I've had many people ask me what they should do. Would going to the wedding endorse the relationship? Would boycotting the wedding communicate that we didn't love them anymore? There are a lot of different views on this issue among good, strong brothers and sisters in Christ. So, given the complexity of this issue, a story on my news feed caught my attention with the headline, "Christian Pastor Dropped by Radio Network Stands by Advice to Grandmother on Attending LGBTQ Wedding."[10]

Come to find out, the pastor in the story is Alistair Begg, a highly respected Bible teacher with a national radio broadcast. I know him personally, and if there is anyone who is confident and courageous about promoting and defending biblical truth, he's among the best.

According to the article, he was asked by a woman if she should attend her grandson's wedding. She didn't know what to do since in her mind it was outside of the boundary of a scriptural view of marriage. After the details were discussed, Alistair told her that it was important that she share with her grandson that as a matter of conscience she could not affirm his decision to proceed with the marriage. But she should assure him, in spite of that, that nothing would ever stop her from loving him. If she made that clear, Alistair told her that she might want to attend the wedding to keep the relationship strong so that she could continue to influence her grandson toward Christ. After all, he mentioned, Jesus did tell us to love our enemies.

After hearing about this conversation, a national radio network that carried his daily Bible teaching ministry immediately canceled his program. And a national pastors conference withdrew the invitation for him to speak because what he had done would be distracting. I was both shocked and disheartened to read of these responses. Here's why . . .

For one thing, while that piece of advice is what other pastors who are deeply committed to God and His Word may have given, once again, we took the sword to one of our own, not for a breach of doctrine but for a matter of discernment that's within the bounds of Christian thought. But second, given that the article was carried in a national news thread that is read by tens of thousands of people, we again gave our nation a good excuse to believe the misguided notion that evangelicals are hateful toward those who identify as LGBTQ+ and that we are willing to punish our own when they seek to differ with us on the details.

In Alistair's message to his congregation explaining why he had counseled the woman the way that he did, he concluded that Christ followers don't affirm gay lifestyles nor do we revile those who identify as LGBTQ+. And both of those responses, as he said, come from our allegiance to the Word of God. Well said, Alistair. Well said!

Issues of Gender

Under the broad heading of human sexuality also comes the contentious issue of gender. Not long ago, few people talked about these topics, but now new terms, new pronouns, and new definitions have been introduced into our parlance. Issues that once would have sounded like fantasy are now hitting home in many communities. Should your local high school allow biological males to play on girls' sports teams? Should your local public library host drag queens reading at the children's story hour? Has your state legislated on transition care for minors? What is the definition of a woman?

All these transitional issues in the territory of what we once thought of as clear lines of demarcation have challenged the biblical reality that it was God's intention that being man and being woman were the non-negotiable assignments. The "God created man in his own image . . . male and female he created them" (Gen. 1:27) reference is now clouded into the promotion of choices that you get to decide. And tragically this notion is introduced into young school children's thought patterns at an early age. While our hearts and a spirit of compassion go out to those who legitimately struggle with gender dysphoria, that is a far cry from the wide-open cultural invitation that anyone can be whoever they want to be.

Clearly, we need to protect our children from ungodly and unhealthy influences that would lead them to confusion, wrong feelings, and harmful choices. We will need to seek Spirit-guided discernment when our place of work requires that we use gender preference pronouns. We should engage efforts to influence our school boards to stop the aggressive promotion of gender choice to our students. And we need to politically engage the issue when there is the opportunity to enact appropriate legislation.

Standing with confidence and courage in times like these is a challenge. But in the end it will validate our claim to be people of a different kingdom with a different King whose truth is eternal and whose love is unlimited.

PRO-LIFE CHALLENGES

After the Supreme Court overturned *Roe v. Wade* in a ruling that turned the issue over to individual states, pro-life advocates rejoiced in what they felt had been a great victory.[11] What actually happened was not what the pro-life movement had hoped for.

The decision raised the issue to a fever pitch with pro-choice sentiment winning the day nationally. In the mid-term elections of 2022, abortion became the leading issue in many states, and many politicians who ran on a pro-life platform were soundly defeated. It now seems to have unleashed a tide of sympathy for pro-choice positions, which has turned up the heat on pro-lifers, long accused of denying a woman autonomy over her own body. The right to an abortion has even more vehemently been linked to women's health.[12]

Many Christians (and others) have a history of massive efforts through the years to rescue the lives of the unborn and to care for women facing an unexpected pregnancy they do not feel ready for. Many have spent hours praying at abortion clinics. We have campaigned and financially supported efforts to elect pro-life candidates and to legislate pro-life policies. We have organized grassroots strategies to raise the awareness of the average citizen to the value of the lives of the unborn. And in addition, literally thousands of pro-life pregnancy support centers have arrived on the scene nationwide to offer an alternative, a real choice, including practical help and support for pregnant women.

But in spite of these efforts, it now feels like we are trying to stem the tide with a pitchfork. And it's a tide that feels more like a tsunami with no assurance that the waters will soon recede.

In my home state of Michigan, the 2022 election saw abortion sympathizers take the governorship and both state houses. Given that majority, the governor advanced Michigan Proposal #3, a ballot initiative that enshrined abortion rights in the state's constitution. This quickly led to the elimination of a host of existing laws protecting both women and their unborn children. This extreme measure also led to the legalization of abortions with no limit regarding term. The proposal also holds within its breadth of interpretation the possibility of greatly hampering or even closing all the lifesaving pregnancy centers in the state if they refuse to provide or refer for abortions.

The sobering reality is that Proposal #3 was passed by a strong majority of voters in spite of the millions of dollars spent in advertisements that clearly explained the serious ramifications of supporting the measure. In light of these threatening realities in Michigan, Jim Sprague, who leads the highly effective Pregnancy Resource Center here in Grand Rapids, is actively building a statewide coalition of pregnancy centers to mutually encourage one another and to lobby for the rights of pregnancy centers to continue to provide the alternative of life in a culture of infant death. One of these organizations is Alpha Grand Rapids, which provides services to both women and men who are facing an unplanned pregnancy.

Ministering in these troubling waters, undeterred servants of life at places like Alpha Grand Rapids offer a wide range of caring alternatives to abortion. Led by Colleen Geisel, AGR creatively sets the pace for comprehensive support of mothers and fathers who have been affected by unplanned pregnancy. The ministry offers medical support through pregnancy tests and ultrasounds, which allow women to bond with their unborn child while receiving compassionate information and resources that address their concerns about continuing the pregnancy. Beyond medical services, AGR also provides ongoing support and resources through one-on-one mentoring, parenting support groups, and educational classes including pregnancy education, parenting classes, GED completion, job skills training, and English as a Second Language. By participating in programs, parents earn items such as diapers, formula, clothing, and other necessities. All of these services work together to not only empower women to choose life for their unborn children, but also to equip them for success in parenting and life in general.

Realizing that part of ongoing success relies on the men who are becoming fathers, the AGR team opened Alpha Men's Center in 2021 as the first standalone building in the United States to comprehensively serve dads. The programs at the Men's Center mimic the programs provided through the Women's Center, giving men access to a supportive community, relevant education, and the tools necessary to thrive as an individual, father, partner, and member of the community. All of the programs through both centers are rooted in faith, so the women and men who attend will be introduced to Christ for the first time or find opportunities to deepen their relationship with Christ through their connection to AGR.

As you can imagine, Alpha Grand Rapid's model of care has caught the attention of the community at large. Colleen and other team members frequently provide tours and have conversations with people who would not identify as pro-life or even as believers, yet multiple people have had responses like, "I don't consider myself pro-life, but I absolutely believe in what you are doing at Alpha." Some have even, of their own accord, become donors to the ministry. By focusing on loving people well and providing compassionate comprehensive care to people regardless of their circumstances, AGR melts the hostility that is often leveled against the pro-life movement. It's a public testimony to the fact that Jesus' people do these kinds of things!

If we really care about the unborn *and* their parents, we should be raving fans of ministries like the ministries that Jim and Colleen lead.

We should be quick to volunteer. To write checks to empower them to expand their influence. To pray for them and personally encourage them. I sometimes wonder if we as evangelicals would have poured our money into solutions like these centers instead of investing in political candidates and campaigns that in the end have failed, we may have been much further down the road on saving the lives of the unborn.

COMPASSION: SEEKING THE LOST

Facing these tensions and their resultant pressures does not excuse us from having a sense of compassion for the lost. I think that it is easy for us to lump all who are proponents of progressive values as a part of the force that is against us. From the people next door whose yard signs betray their progressive political preference to the people we work with who discuss politics at the water cooler to the guys at the golf club who talk about preferred progressive candidates . . . they are nonetheless people whom God loves and whom God pursues to offer them a better way. And we may just be the ones to show them that way.

Matthew tells us that when Jesus saw the masses, He was moved with compassion, because they were like sheep without a shepherd (Matt. 9:36). We live in a sinful world. As believers, we live among sinners, also being sinful though redeemed by Christ. And Jesus has called us to pursue the lost with His love—not to demonize them. While clinging to the truth with confidence and courage means that we don't endorse the wrong ways of our world, being found in the way with Jesus does require that we have a loving, Christlike attitude toward those He came to pursue and save.

If that thought makes you uncomfortable, then you probably haven't read Luke 15 recently. In fact, even a casual reading of the Gospels demonstrates that His mission was one of redemption and restoration, that He had come to seek and to save that which was lost. As Jesus said in John 3:17, "For God did not send his Son into the world to condemn the world, but in order that the world might be saved through him." And He lived that out in spite of rising criticism from religious people who opposed Him.

Luke tells us that on one occasion Jesus was seen with tax collectors and sinners. This annoyed the Pharisees who were "grumbling," as Luke says, because "this man receives sinners and eats with them" (Luke 15:1). If you were a tax collector in Jewish society, you were the low guy on the totem pole of moral decency. You had sold yourself out to the oppressive ruling powers of Rome and collected their exorbitant taxes.

And then there were the bottom feeders, the "sinners," who lived outside the rules and regulations of the religious establishment. To Jews of His day, both categories represented the worst kinds of people in society. And Jesus was caught red-handed hanging with the wrong crowd. But instead of apologizing—"Yeah, you're right. What was I thinking?"—and extracting Himself from such company, Jesus told three stories to explain why He spent time with people like this. They were stories about the lost: a lost lamb, lost coins, and a lost son, all told in Luke 15.

The History of Lostness

Lostness has an important history. In the beginning, God's prized creation, Adam and Eve, ruled His garden and lived in unhindered fellowship with Him and with each other. Adam and Eve had the distinct honor of being created in His image so that there could be intimacy with God and a fellowship that God could enjoy as they lived to glorify Him. Adam and Eve were the supreme highlight of creation, God's special image-bearing pair! Enter Satan to lure them away from God and leave them to themselves in the domain of darkness.

At this point in biblical history, God suffers a significant loss. He has lost His loving companions who guard and oversee the kingdom of His garden. His options? Annihilate all that He had created and start again or seek to recover the loss by restoring fallen humanity to His fellowship. He chose restoration, as is seen when Jesus walked back into the garden to redeem and restore those first lost sinners (see Gen. 3). That loss and God's desire to reclaim His significant loss is the metanarrative of Scripture. It is the reason Jesus walked back into the fallen garden of our world two thousand years ago. It is the reason He is found in Luke 15 in the company of lost people.

The stories He tells unlock the importance of living to seek the lost.

First, in each of the stories the lost commodities all have worth and value. Sheep were a measure of wealth and as such were of high value to a shepherd. A woman's coins had immense value to her. They would have been her social security fund. And what can we say about the value of a lost son? The stories remind us that even sinners are of value to God. He has lost what He loves and seeks to restore them to fellowship with Him. And given that sinners, like the original pair, are worthy of God's pursuit, we too should share in His redemptive agenda.

Second, in each of the stories the lost commodities are hopelessly and helplessly lost without intervention. Any shepherd will tell you that sheep do not return to the fold at night on their own. Lost coins don't suddenly reappear. And rebellious sons don't return to fellowship without the intervention of a forgiving father. The coming of Jesus is the ultimate intervention. As we have noted, He came to seek and save the lost. He came to pursue us. And then said, "As the Father has sent me, even so I am sending you" (John 20:21).

> God, in His amazing grace, is the restorer of the lost. He watches for us to come. He receives us with open arms!

Third, the prodigal's offense was not the naughty things he did in the far country, although for a Jewish boy they *were* pretty despicable. His real offense was against his father. In Jewish Orthodox culture, even to this day, if a son asks for his inheritance ahead of time it is like saying to your father, "I wish you were dead." It is the worst thing a son could do to his dad. This account reminds us that the offense of sinners is not an offense against us. We need to stop taking things personally. Sinners offend God. And it is His responsibility to deal with them, and our responsibility to lovingly seek them. In the end, if they repent and come home, we can be assured that God is waiting to welcome them and to throw a celebration with the best robe, the best ring, and the menu feature of a fatted calf!

This was a shocking conclusion to those who were listening to the parable. This was actually a common story that Jewish parents would tell their children to scare them into never doing such a thing to their family. The story would end with the boy coming home and getting punished by his dad. But Jesus stunned His listeners with a turn of the tale. The father of the boy was watching and waiting for the prodigal to return home. And when he saw his son, he ran to embrace him and to restore him completely to family fellowship. God, in His amazing grace, is the restorer of the lost. He watches for us to come. He receives us with open arms, and all of heaven breaks out in a joyous refrain—for which we can all be thankful!

"Let Light Shine Out of Darkness"

A woman I know has run a ministry to exotic dancers. Clubs where these dancers entertain aren't typically places Christians would go to, and these entertainers are among those "a good Christian" wouldn't want to be seen with.

But God laid a burden on this person's heart for these women. Many of them have been trafficked and are in the grips of addiction under the tyrannical thumb of the pimps who run the clubs. So, unconcerned about who might think that a good Christian girl should have nothing to do with an industry like that, she would go into the clubs and meet the girls, bake cookies, and offer to help in any way possible. Over time, as she built relationships with them, they began to trust and confide in her. She took them on retreats where she shared the gospel and encouraged them spiritually.

Today, by God's grace, some of them have found honorable employment elsewhere. They have come to know Jesus as their Lord and are building lives from a new beginning. This compassionate woman went to seek and to save the lost. She saw value in each of these women, knowing that they were created in the image of God and that God loved them. She intervened in their lives at a risk to her own reputation with a message of freedom and restoration. A lot of those former dancers are really thankful that she went to "hang out with sinners" just as Jesus did!

We need to remind ourselves that drawing swords against sinners was not Christ's way. Hanging out with them was.

I regret to tell you that I have not always done this well. For several years, Martie and I spent some time in the English countryside where I would do some writing and escape the business in the fast track of life in Chicago. Our prayer was that while there we could find ways to be a witness for Christ.

In our small village, a group of guys would go to the local pub for a pint every Thursday. I knew some of them well and I'm quite certain that they would have welcomed me to join them. But at that point in my thinking, having a pint with them was not the right thing to do. So, I never went. Reflecting back on that, having a pint was not a doctrinal issue or even a biblical issue, but I was held back by the rules of the "system." Rules that said that guys like me, the president of Moody no less, should not be imbibing. I think of what might have happened if I could have been there with them while they discussed life and its issues. It would have been a great opportunity to interject Jesus into the situation when appropriate. It seems to me that I missed an important chance to build a bridge that Jesus could walk across.

Of course, compassionately befriending sinners does not mean that we do the things they do when they cross the line of what clearly is wrong. But it does mean that spending time with them and living in ways that raise their curiosity opens their hearts to what we have to say.

We need to remind ourselves that drawing swords against sinners was not Christ's way. Hanging out with them was. And quite frankly, we hang out with all kinds of people every day. People who are different than we are. People who think and believe differently than we do. Who act differently than we do. Who hold divergent political and social opinions from ours. People who at times don't like us and all that we stand for. Yet these are people who have worth and value to God. We work with them. We go to school with them. We shop in stores where they are shopping. We live next door to them. Some are in our family. Relating to them in ways that reflect the love of God is a great opportunity to start spending time with them in a redemptive way!

─────── TO THINK ABOUT ───────

Can you think of a time when the cultural shift caused you to respond with confidence and courage? What was the nature of your attitude in your response? What opportunities have you taken to build compassionate, positive relationships with those who are outside of the kingdom regardless of their lifestyles or political positions?

FOUR

WHOSE KINGDOM?

....

He has delivered us from the domain of darkness
and transferred us to the kingdom of his beloved Son.

COLOSSIANS 1:13

If you've traveled to foreign countries, you know that citizens of those cultures have certain characteristics that identify them as being a part of the nation they call home. Their language, their styles of dress, their way of thinking, the sports they like, the food they eat, are all reflections of their nationality. Those who belong to the kingdom of Christ have markers in their lives that make their identity clear: markers that are uniquely different than the lives of those who belong to an earthly kingdom.

KINGDOM PEOPLE

In one description of the characteristics of kingdom people living in a hostile environment, Paul opens the letter to Christians in Colossae by telling them that he is praying that they will be known for five kingdom markers (Col. 1:10–12). Paul's prayer is that they will do the following:

Live lives worthy of our Lord. "Worthy" would certainly mean worthy of His conquering victory by living with a winning perspective on life. Lives worthy of Him live out the values of His kingdom as prescribed in the Sermon on the Mount and the various life-transforming principles that He taught: loving our enemies, living to serve and bless others, being generous to the poor and needy, bringing hope and healing to the unclean of our communities. And living with the confidence and courage that comes from remembering that He is the conquering King.

Be strong, not weak and fearful. Intimidation is not in the vocabulary of kingdom people. Our King through His resurrection has defeated death, our strongest enemy, and sentenced the evil prince of this world to eternal judgment! We live in that strength.

Persistently endure. As Jesus said, the establishment of His kingdom on earth is a long-term adventure, starting small and growing slowly like a mustard seed becoming a tree (Matt. 13:31–32). For the early Christians, as for us, it takes endurance. And it should be noted that the early church took three centuries to change their world by their routine faithfulness to the ways of Jesus. Changed lives and bulging congregations throughout those three centuries showed the world an attractive alternative to the emptiness and chaotic ways of the godforsaken culture in which they lived.

Be known for joy. The word used for joy in the Bible is not 24/7 happiness. It is a deep, settled sense that all is well, regardless. Dallas Willard has famously described joy as "a pervasive sense of well-being that is infused with hope because of the goodness of God." If you are a privileged citizen of Christ's kingdom, then no matter what is happening around your life in the moment you can embrace this kind of joy.

Be known for thankful lives. When you think of all the realities that God graciously supplies in His kingdom—especially when you compare them to the dark and destructive outcomes of life in the earthly kingdom, which Paul calls "the domain of darkness"—you suddenly awake to not only a sense of joy but of thankfulness as well.

Walk in the worthy ways of our conquering King. Be strong. Persistently endure. Be joyful. Be thankful. Notice the dramatic difference of these kingdom markers to the losing, hopeless attitudes we are prone to embrace when we focus our attention singularly on the earthbound kingdom around us.

It's important to reflect on our own actions and attitudes in light of what Paul has outlined. In the face of growing hostility, could it be said that we are known for responding to our culture with Christ-honoring lives? In our attitudes and actions, do we present a posture of godly strength? Are we persisting without wavering in lives that are clearly joyful and thankful?

So the question is, how do we pivot to actions and attitudes that demonstrate to a watching world that we are different? Attractively different. That we belong to a different kingdom.

KINGDOM LOCATION

We know that when it comes to real estate, three things matter: location, location, location. It's the same with us. In our text, Paul goes on to say that the motivation and the reason for living lives that reflect kingdom virtues is that we are no longer located in "the domain of darkness," but that God has "rescued us from the domain of darkness and transferred us to the kingdom of his beloved Son" (Col. 1:13).

This transfer is the biggest relocation project in history, at the cost of the shed blood of Jesus, "in whom we have redemption, the forgiveness of sins" (v. 14). Paul in essence has reminded us that we are no longer citizens of the kingdom of this world, but that our new location is in Jesus' kingdom, which makes all the difference in who we are and what we do.

At the end of the day there are only two kingdoms: the kingdom of Satan and the kingdom of Christ. Contrasting the distinctives of the two kingdoms should make us joyful and thankful to be included in His kingdom.

Satan's kingdom is characterized as the domain of darkness. Darkness is the realm where fear, danger, confusion, disorientation, and evil reside.

Jesus' kingdom is characterized by light. Jesus entered the realm of darkness and announced that He is the "light of the world" (John 8:12). And He turned on the lights for us, chasing away the dangers and disorientation of the darkness.

Satan's kingdom is a kingdom of death. Jesus told the religious leaders of His day that they were of their father the devil, who was a murderer from the beginning (John 8:44). Every abortion. Every suicide. Every act of genocide. Every war. Every pandemic is cause for celebration in hell.

Jesus' kingdom is a kingdom where righteousness, peace, and joy prevail. It's about shalom. Peace, order, and justice.

Jesus' kingdom is a kingdom of life. As He said, "I am the way, and the truth, and the life" (John 14:6). It's an abundant, eternal life that He shares with all who come to Him!

Satan's kingdom is a kingdom of lies. There is no truth in him (John 8:44). His kingdom is about deceit and deception, lying to us about our sexuality, power, self-advancement, wealth, pleasure, and a host of other pursuits.

Jesus' kingdom is a kingdom of truth. Jesus made this bold claim: "I am the truth!" (John 14:6). Jesus shames the destructive lies of our enemy and gives us reliable truth upon which we can build our lives with confidence and prosper.

Satan's kingdom is a kingdom that dispenses quantities of unrighteousness, conflict, and sorrow.

Jesus' kingdom is a kingdom where righteousness, peace, and joy prevail (Rom. 14:17).

Satan's kingdom is a kingdom of chaos. Everywhere Satan shows up, chaos is present.

Jesus' kingdom is about shalom. Peace, order, and justice.

Satan's kingdom is temporal.

Jesus' kingdom is eternal.

Satan's kingdom is defeated, which reminds us that it's our earth-bound culture that is the ultimate loser, headed for extinction.

Jesus' kingdom is victorious. It is the citizens of His kingdom who flourish since we are not the losers, but we belong to an emerging world order that is eternally victorious.

To which kingdom would you rather belong?

What a relief to know we are citizens of His kingdom and that we have been transplanted into the kingdom of God's dear Son. A kingdom that lights up the darkness; brings life in the place of death; shames the lies with truth; brings harmony to chaos; righteousness, peace, and joy to its citizens; and a kingdom that is ultimately eternally victorious. A victory that was guaranteed by an empty tomb that damned the domain of darkness.

A victory that we celebrate every Easter. Easter is the ultimate contrast between the kingdoms of Satan and of Christ. Christ's kingdom celebrates that love has won over hate; hope has won over despair; and for all eternity, life has won over death!

KINGDOM VICTORY

When our children were younger, they would periodically bring home from school a word that would shock us all. I always had to remind them that that word might be used on the school playground by others, but we didn't use it in our family; it wasn't in our family's vocabulary. Likewise, given our privileged position in His kingdom, words like *defeat* and *despair* are not in our vocabulary! They don't show up in the kingdom dictionary.

It's important for us to remember that for kingdom people life is like a feature-length film with God as the executive producer. Freeze-framing it in this moment of cultural demise and the resultant hostility toward followers raises all the wrong attitudes and diverts us to wrong actions. But knowing that God is the executive producer, we let the film roll to its full-length conclusion, which ends in the glorious victory of Jesus who ushers in the fullness of His eternal kingdom in a new heaven and earth. As John says,

> Then I saw a new heaven and a new earth, for the first heaven and the first earth had passed away, and the sea was no more. And I saw the holy city, new Jerusalem, coming down out of heaven from God, prepared as a bride adorned for her husband. And I heard a loud voice from the throne saying, "Behold, the dwelling place of God is with man. He will dwell with them, and they will be his people, and God himself will be with them as their God. He will wipe away every tear from their eyes, and death shall be no more, neither shall there be mourning, nor crying, nor pain anymore, for the former things have passed away."
>
> And he who was seated on the throne said, "Behold, I am making all things new." Also he said, "Write this down, for these words are trustworthy and true." And he said to me, "It is done! I am the Alpha and the Omega, the beginning and the end." (Rev. 21:1–6)

For me, just reading these words is a therapeutic exercise in attitude adjustment!

A few Christmases ago Martie and I had the privilege of hearing Handel's *Messiah* sung by a five-hundred-voice choir, accompanied by the London Symphony Orchestra in London's Royal Albert Hall. The hall was packed to capacity with a crowd of five thousand. It was a powerful performance, highlighted by a rousing rendition of the "Hallelujah Chorus." As everyone stood, a long-standing tradition, the choir ramped up the energy and, with the symphony and pipe organ weighing in with equal enthusiasm, sang the repeated lines, "King of Kings and Lord of

Lords, and He shall reign forever and ever! King of Kings and Lord of Lords, and He shall reign forever and ever, forever and ever, forever and ever! Hallelujah!" There in the heart of that pagan city, with five thousand on their feet, Jesus was being hailed as the eternal King! I could hardly restrain the tears of joy. They were singing about my King, about *the* King!

Jesus' words to His disheartened disciples who were about ready to face a hostile world without Him are instructive about how His victorious reign transforms our mood and the way we respond. He says, "In this world you will have tribulation" (John 16:33). So why should we be surprised when trouble comes from a hostile culture? But He surprisingly concludes (and here I like the King James Version a lot), "But be of good cheer; I have overcome the world."

We need to remind ourselves often that as kingdom people living in the long view, we have a lot to cheer about! I love the affirming lyrics to the song "Reign Above It All." Songwriter Paul McClure skillfully expresses how no name is higher, that Jesus reigns above everything, and declares that all of heaven and earth should "erupt in song!"[13] This is how we understand the long view—by knowing, and trusting, and rejoicing in the eventual victory.

KINGDOM KNOWLEDGE

In Colossians 1, Paul writes that it is his prayer that kingdom people will be "filled with the knowledge of his will in all spiritual wisdom and understanding" (Col. 1:9). This raises the question, "In the face of our cultural challenges, what would His will be?"

This is challenging territory because it's easy to let our instincts determine what would be the best way to respond to the downward drift. I've learned that when I am confronted with a decision on how to act and react, I need to pause and be sure that my responses are truly reflective of His ways and not my own. I've come to realize that given my fallenness, my first instincts are usually wrong. If you offend me, my first instinct is not to forgive, love, pray for you, and bless you! Which, by the way, is His will for me (Matt. 5:43–48). Pausing is important because Scripture advises us that His thoughts are not our thoughts and that His ways are not our ways (Isa. 55:8). Scripture warns us that there are ways that seem right to us but in the end they are destructive (Prov. 14:12), which is why Scripture encourages us not to lean on our own understanding but to let Him direct our paths (Prov. 3:5–6).

> *It is we who are upside down, and He has come to turn us right side up.*

So considering how to respond in this often hostile culture we need to be sure we are responding in sync with His wisdom and His ways. We should keep in mind that a what-comes-naturally response most likely is not His way. The psalmist prayed, "Make me to know *your* ways, O LORD; teach me *your* paths" (Ps. 25:4).

The ways of Jesus will seem upside down to us. Like, if you want to live you have to die to yourself. If you want to gain, you need to give it away. Love your enemy. Turn the other cheek. It all seems so unnatural, so out of order. But we need to realize that He is not the one who is upside down. As victims of the fall, we are the broken ones, and our natural instincts are usually flawed. It is we who are upside down and He has come to turn us right side up so that we can reflect the right-side-upness of His kingdom in all that we do—including how we live in our culture.

As kingdom people we have an identity that transforms our lives to reflect the worthiness of His kingdom.

KINGDOM IDENTITY

If you and I had coffee together, just the two of us, and I asked you to tell me a little about yourself, I wonder what you would say. I might hear something about your occupation or your position in life: student, parent, athlete, and so on. If I asked you about your religion, answers like Baptist, Anglican, Presbyterian might be supplied. And your politics? I might hear Republican, Democrat, or Independent as the answer to your political identity.

But in the end, none of these answers is the right answer to your true identity as a kingdom recruit. And, I should add, my question is not a throwaway question. How we perceive ourselves often dictates how we live. My dad was a pastor, so I grew up as a PK (pastor's kid). Given my propensity to get into trouble, no one in my dad's church ever said PK with a smile on their face. I would often hear, "Young man" (I knew I was in trouble when they started like that), "you're the pastor's son. You should be an example to the other kids!" I didn't want to be an example—I was only five! But their strategy to change my behavioral patterns was to get me to embrace a new identity that would be transformative in my life.

One of my favorite stories from British politics is told about former prime minister Margaret Thatcher, who, when running for office, visited a retirement home. She was greeted with great delight by all the residents except for a woman sitting in the corner, totally disengaged. Finally, Thatcher went over to greet her personally. The woman simply gazed past Mrs. Thatcher, totally unconnected to the moment.

Thatcher finally said, "Do you know who I am?"

The woman came to and said, "No, but that nurse over there helps us with those kinds of things."

Thankfully Jesus helps us with this kind of thing, with who we are in our kingdom identity!

When He saw Peter and Andrew casting their nets into the sea, Jesus called to them and said, "Follow me, and I will make you fishers of men." In fact, throughout the gospels when Jesus is in recruiting mode, He consistently calls people to "follow" Him. So if, over that cup of coffee, you would have answered, "Joe, thanks for asking, I am a follower of

Jesus!" that would have been spot on. Being a follower of Jesus is the core identity of His kingdom people—an identity that transforms and defines all that we are and do.

A rabbi in the time of Jesus would have a group of followers. Being a follower was a privileged position in that culture. Followers lived in community with the rabbi, sat under his teaching, and with great admiration for their rabbi would often emulate him in their attitudes and actions. To fishermen, becoming a follower was a step up that they couldn't resist. It's no wonder that the text tells us that "immediately they left their nets and followed him" (Matt. 4:18–22). But what would that mean? In what ways would that transform and define them? When "fishermen" was their identity, they acted like, worked like, marketed like, and fished like fishermen. What would the new identity do to reflect that they were followers of Jesus?

The Greek word in the Matthew text is *akoloutheo*, which means to be found in the way with, or "to walk the same road."[14] For them, their new life would be lived in the ways of Jesus—lived in the ways of the one who boldly claimed, "I am the way" (John 14:6). I love to think of Jesus in these terms. Way-maker Jesus. Path-treader Jesus. The Jesus who came into our world and refused to walk in the heavily trafficked, deeply rutted ways of fallen humanity. These ways have a warning sign at their trailhead that says, "There is a way that seems right to you but in it are the ways of death" (see Prov. 16:25). Rejecting the allure of these destructive ways, Jesus took the machete of His wisdom and cut new and unusual ways through the jungle of human affairs, revealing His kingdom paths and recruiting ordinary people like you and me to walk in those ways with Him.

For instance, as we have noted before, Matthew 5:43 records His will when He said, "You have heard that it was said, 'You shall love your neighbor and hate your enemy.'" That'd be the natural inclination, taking the well-trodden road of bitterness, revenge, and hate. Instead, He said, "But *I* say to you, Love your enemies and pray for those who persecute you, so that you may be sons of your Father who is in heaven." (Note: whenever He says, "but *I* say to you," it's the sound of His machete cutting a whole new path.) Is anyone reading this thankful that God has loved His enemies? And Jesus walked that path all the way to the cross. I wonder if you and I are walking in this way with Him.

> *If you want to be great in My kingdom, He stressed, you need to live your life as a servant. The way up is down.*

To disciples who were clamoring for power and places of influence in the coming kingdom, He explained that was the way the Gentiles operate, lording it over others, "but it shall not be so among you" (Matt. 20:20–28). If you want to be great in My kingdom, He stressed, you need to live your life as a servant. The way up is down.

To a bystander who asked Jesus to tell his brother to divide the inheritance with him, Jesus told him to stop walking in the way of greed because, as Jesus said, "Take care, and be on your guard against all covetousness, for one's life does not consist in the abundance of his possessions." He went on to explain the difference between someone who collects treasure for himself or herself rather than being rich in the ways of God (Luke 12:13–21).

MY WAY OR THE KINGDOM HIGHWAY

The list of the ways of our King in His kingdom is long, and at times challenging. But they are the ways that give us openings for the good news in our dark world.

Dead-end way: An eye for an eye! Return evil for evil!

Jesus' way: Turn the other cheek.

Dead-end way: Don't get mad, just get even!

Jesus' way: Love your enemies.

Dead-end way: Clamor for power and position!

Jesus' way: Consider yourself to be a servant.

Dead-end way: Live to get and gain as much as you can!

Jesus' way: Store up treasure in heaven.

Dead-end way: Marginalize those who aren't like you!

Jesus' way: Welcome all into the warmth of your love.

Dead-end way: Resist anything that would cause suffering or discomfort!

Jesus' way: Take up your cross and follow Me!

Dead-end way: Give people what they deserve!

Jesus' way: Be a dispenser of grace and mercy.

Dead-end way: Love when it is safe!

Jesus' way: Love when it is costly.

Dead-end way: Love when it is deserved!

Jesus' way: Love regardless.

Dead-end way: Live for self!

Jesus' way: Live for the benefit of others.

Dead-end way: Forgive sparingly!

Jesus' way: Forgive seventy-seven times.

The list of the ways in which followers live is long, often challenging, but always right! They are the ways of His kingdom and the ways that followers validate their claim to be legitimate disciples.

And these are the ways we influence our culture for Christ and His kingdom. Early Christians did this so well that six times in Acts the public refers to them as people of "the Way." And, when Paul was before the high-ranking government official Felix, on trial in Caesarea Maritima, it is said that Felix had "a rather accurate knowledge of the Way" (Acts 24:22). Could it be that we would live so in the ways of Jesus that people around us would be familiar with "the Way"?

These are the ways we influence our culture for Christ and His kingdom.

Escaping the cruel winter of Michigan one year, I met a fellow vacationer only to find out that we had grown up in the same town and gone to the same high school. In the course of our conversation, he asked me, "What was your name again?"

I said Joe Stowell.

He replied, "Oh, I thought you said Stilwell. I have a client by that name."

Interestingly enough, in my dad's church there was a Stilwell family, and one of the sons was Art Stilwell, who owned a large car dealership. I said, "Art Stilwell?"

Unbelievably, the attorney said, "Yes. I have no other client like Art!"

When I inquired as to why he said that, he went on, "Most of my clients who want me to help them say I should do anything possible to resolve the issue in their favor. But when I ask Art what he wants me to do he always says, 'Do what's honorable and right.'" And then the man kind of shook his head and raised his eyebrows in an admiring sort of way and repeated, "I have no other client like Art."

Art showed him what people of the Way are like. Is it possible that Art planted a seed of the gospel in that attorney's heart that would later be harvested to the glory of God?

The temptation will be to want to claim to be a follower but to find it more comfortable, less troublesome, to live in our own ways. To live by our natural instincts. To respond to our culture in ways that come naturally.

A friend of mine was in the process of leaving his wife to marry his executive assistant with whom he was having an affair. Two of his other friends and I met up with him, with the goal of getting him back into "the Way." I said to him, "If you go through with this, don't ever tell anyone that you are a follower of Jesus, as that would shame the name of Christ." He replied, "Oh, but I am a follower of Jesus!"

His statement was delusional. When it comes to being a follower you can't have it both ways. Followers stay in the path with Him! Paths that revolutionize the way that we live. Claiming to be a follower yet living in our own ways will always bring shame to His name and defeat our ability to attract others to the good life that only Jesus can give.

KINGDOM EXCELLENCIES

Living negatively in our own ways of responding to the culture, as we have said, is not an effective way to attract others to Christ. Would they really want to be like us given our less than admirable attitudes and actions? I doubt it.

In a recent poll conducted by the Pew Research Center, evangelicals were regarded as the most unfavorable religious subculture in America.[15] No doubt some may think it is because of our stands for morality in relation to the moral decline in America. But interestingly, Catholics and Mormons, who for the most part share our convictions on moral issues, are more favorably viewed than evangelicals, according to the survey. It is not unreasonable to conclude that it is because we are not all that likable.

Trying to make disciples with our losing attitudes and misguided political posturing is a losing proposition. This is why Peter, writing to persecuted believers in the first century reminds them that as kingdom people they are "a chosen race, a royal priesthood, a holy nation, a people for his own possession" for the purpose of living lives that "proclaim the excellencies of him who has called you out of darkness into his marvelous light" (1 Peter 2:9).

What was it that made Him so attractive to the masses who followed Him wherever He went? Why did they hang on every word? What was so excellent about Him?

He offered hope to the rejected and unclean. In a world where religious leaders despised sinners, he told sinners that God was a loving and forgiving God by making the father in the story of the prodigal a welcoming Father. He communicated love to those who had been disposed as valueless, like lepers and demoniacs. And He elevated the value of women. He offered inclusion to the canceled. He advocated for forgiven prostitutes who were the targets of religious people's scorn. He rejected ascending to places of prestigious power and instead sided with the common man and woman and lived as a servant toward others.

In a world that was characterized by the chaos of class warfare, ethnic pride and prejudice, oppression and exclusion, He was different. Dramatically different. Attractively different.

He said that everyone was welcome in His kingdom regardless of color, class, or culture. He was loving, patient, hopeful, merciful, truthful, grace-filled, forgiving, peace-extending, and a healer. In a world that was characterized by the chaos of class warfare, ethnic pride and prejudice, oppression and exclusion, He was different. Dramatically different. Attractively different. He epitomized what people were longing for. He was authentic. The list of His excellencies, His attractive attitudes and actions, is long and impressive.

It's those excellencies lived out through our lives in routine faithfulness that give us opportunities to attract others to Jesus. We'd know that we were making some progress if pagans would say, "I don't get these

Christians but all the ones I know are really, really good people. And our world would be a better place if more of us were like them." When people start talking like this about us, we may be close to an opportunity to introduce them to the one who showed us how to live. We just may be close to influencing our culture for Christ.

. . . .

Brian Keepers, pastor of Trinity Reformed Church in Orange City, Iowa, has it right when he says, "We need to show the world another way, a better way. A way that holds together truth *and* grace, justice *and* kindness, conviction *and* humility, and faithfully points to another king and kingdom."[16]

By God's grace, may our lives present the beauty of the gospel in the compelling way that these early Christians did. May we light the darkness with the excellencies of His name. May all who come in contact with us see the power of the gospel in its full force in our attitudes and actions, as we welcome their weary souls to find their rest in Him.

———— TO THINK ABOUT ————

When you think of Paul's five kingdom markers, which ones reflect your attitude given the increasing darkness that we live in? Do you embrace the ramifications of identifying as a follower of Jesus? Are you willing to walk in His ways in response to the cultural drift? Can you think of a time when you showed your world a better way?

FIVE

BACK TO THE FUTURE!

. . . .

Let us hold fast to the confession of our hope without wavering,
for he who promised is faithful.

HEBREWS 10:23

One of the attractive qualities, the excellencies, of early Christians was that they were hopeful people. Amazingly, they maintained their hopefulness in the midst of dire, far-less-than-hopeful circumstances. They were stellar examples of the "living hope" Peter calls us to (1 Peter 1:3).

I have a long list of my all-time favorite sporting events. Near the top of the list is the 1980 Winter Olympics that was held at Lake Placid, New York. To grasp the significance of this event, you need to remember the global and national context. Globally, Russia was seen as a constant threat with its military might and nuclear power. Iran was holding a dozen of our citizens as hostages and, in an effort to free them, our special forces military helicopters crashed in the desert on the way to the rescue. Back home, interest rates were in the double digits and our president, Jimmy Carter, told us that America was in a "malaise."

We had little if anything to cheer about as Americans. And now our teams in the Olympics, particularly our hockey team, were about to be humiliated on the world stage. Our hockey team drew a match with the team from our global adversary, the Soviet Union. It was back when professional athletes could not participate in the Olympics. So it would be our best college players against state-sponsored athletes from the Soviet Union, many of whom I feared would be on steroids or other game-enhancing substances. It looked like further humiliation for America was in the making.

> *I watched the replay of the game with a radically different attitude. I knew who would win in the end.*

I recall coming home and turning on the TV to see how the hockey game was going. To my amazement, they were in the second period, and the game was tied! I had expected us to be in a serious deficit by the second period. I sat down to watch the remainder of the game. Though I had paid for the whole couch, I only used the front third and anxiously followed every move of our team, all the while knowing that at any moment Russia would explode and bury us by several goals. It was a nail-biter, and until the very end I feared the worst. But to my amazement, our underdog hockey team beat the Russians and eventually went on two days later to win the gold medal!

The win was so significant that the networks rebroadcast the game for all who missed it in the first place. I couldn't wait to watch it from start to finish. Only this time it was different. I settled back and used the whole couch. Popcorn in hand and a Coke on the table next to me and feet up on the hassock, I watched the game with a radically different attitude. What made the difference? Same game. Same plays. Same players. The difference was that I knew how the game would finish. I knew who would win in the end.

"CHIN UP" PEOPLE IN A PESSIMISTIC WORLD

In a sense, we live in nail-biting times as followers of Christ, feeling that we are in a losing battle with forces beyond our control. Not knowing what to do, our anxieties show up in sometimes less-than-hopeful ways as we watch the world gain increasing traction against all that we hold dear.

By contrast, early Christians remained hopeful in spite of their circumstances. Knowing their privileged place in the kingdom, they walked worthy of their Lord with heads held high as they persisted with joy and thanksgiving. They were the "chin up" people. They held tenaciously to what they believed, even in the face of cultural pressure and the threat of death. They had a compassionate sense of confidence and courage. So what was their secret? Their secret is wrapped up in one word: hope! They knew how the game would end. They were people who believed that God's Word was true and that the future belonged to them. They were driven and defined by the attractive virtue of hopefulness.

They were optimists in a pessimistic world.

But for us, losing hope is a regular event. Every time our favorite candidate loses an election, we lose hope. Every time the Supreme Court votes against something we value, we lose hope. Whenever we feel socially marginalized, we lose hope. Whenever we read the headlines about the advance of the progressive agenda, we lose hope. In our world there are lots of opportunities for followers of Jesus to lose hope. When we lose hope, we broadcast to those around us that we are the defeated ones. And the world gets the message. In a recent national survey, fewer than 10 percent of adults in the US describe evangelicals as hopeful.[17] In light of that finding, I fear to think of how hard it's going to be to lead those 90 percent of Americans to Jesus.

Could it be that we have deceived ourselves, or is it just that we have forgotten the empty tomb? As we have already noted, we are not the losers. There is no deceit worse than self-deceit. While it may look like we are the defeated ones, we need to remember that life is like football—in the end it makes no difference if the other team has a high-scoring quarter if they lose the whole game. And our hope in the certainty of that reality makes all the difference in our attitudes and how we act as followers of Jesus. Hope is the prize for all followers who live in light of the long view. It's what makes us attractively optimistic and it's the champion that drives out fear, discouragement, and despair.

So let's unwrap what it means to be hopeful followers of Christ.

A CERTAIN HOPE

The way we normally think of hope is not what the Bible means by hope. Hope in our minds is a "maybe" kind of word. We hope that it won't rain on vacation. We hope that the Cubs have a better season next year. We hope we will get a promotion and a raise.

Biblical hope, on the other hand, is grounded in certainty. It refers to the assurance of a future certainty in which we put our trust. A future certainty that ignites confidence and courage in otherwise defeated souls. And, according to the writer of Hebrews, it is faith that triggers this kind of certainty-hope in our lives, "Now faith is the assurance of things hoped for, the conviction of things not seen" (Heb. 11:1).

We sometimes think that a system of belief that is built on faith is less legitimate. But the reality is that every belief system begins with steps of faith. Atheists base their belief system on the assumption that there is no God, which is unprovable. To be an atheist you need to take a step of faith. And so do agnostics. They base their belief system on the assumption that maybe there is and maybe there is not a God. Unprovable as well. The question is, Which step of faith is more reasonable?

For Christians, there are only two steps of faith that we need to trigger the power of the assurance of hope in our lives.

Step #1

Faith in the reality that there is a God who revealed Himself in creation. Martie and I were at a "dark sky" campground recently where there was no light pollution. You could look into the night sky and see the blanket of stars and planets. It was an amazing experience. The Milky Way stretched across the heavens, and the stars were innumerable. Some believe there are as many as 100 billion stars in our galaxy. And to think that there are, according to some estimates, as many as 200 billion galaxies just like ours makes it reasonable to believe that this didn't just happen by accident but that there was someone who designed and sustains it all.

And think of the thousands of species of the animal kingdom from the depths of the sea to the birds of the air. And consider the amazing complexities of our bodies, from the micro design of our DNA to the highly sophisticated functions of our brains. You could spend a lifetime and not be able to plumb the depths and intricacies of all that is around us and within us.

In the end, you would have to say, "Really? These things just happened?" It's not a blind leap into the dark to say there must have been a transcendent designer who put all of this into place and who sustains it in good order. In fact, as it is often said it takes more faith to believe that there isn't a God than to believe that there is. Paul underscores this when he wrote to the church in Rome that there was enough evidence in all of creation to leave those who refuse to believe in God without excuse (see Rom. 1:19–20).

But what would this God be like?

Step #2

Faith in the assurance that He has revealed Himself and His will and His ways in the Bible. The Bible is an amazing book, and denying that it is divinely produced is hard to do in light of its origin. If you could manage the production of a book written over millennia by different people from different cultures who spoke different languages and who had different perspectives, you would produce a collection of disconnected and often contradictory essays that would make little or no sense. Yet the Bible is a coherent narrative, written by different people who lived in different centuries, who spoke different languages, that tells a consistent story from the beginning of time into eternity. This is undeniably supernatural.

Add to that the fact that the prophesies in Scripture have consistently come to fruition, and archaeological discoveries have validated its history. It is not illogical to say that it is a book written and preserved under the direction of a God who wants us to know what He is like and what His will and ways for our life are. And in a wonderful sense, it is a reminder that He just wasn't Creator and controller of all things but that He is a God who cares for us and seeks to redeem and restore us to Himself.

In the end, our faith in God and His Word is a choice. Not a "put your blindfold on and jump into Christianity" kind of choice but a logical, well-supported choice in a system of belief that makes life-altering sense. And when we choose to believe that He is and that He has revealed Himself, His will, and His ways in Scripture, we have certainty of the things that are promised to us. Certainty of what we hope for. A certainty based on the revealed fact that He is faithful and will keep His promises.

HOPE–CERTAINLY!

We have a certain hope in His presence, that He will never leave us or forsake us, and therefore we can confidently say, "The Lord is my helper; I will not fear; what can man do to me?" (Heb. 13:6). Embracing the reality of His constant presence is the antidote to fear.

We have a certain hope that no matter what comes our way in terms of suffering or persecution, He has the power to work all things together for our good and His glory (see Rom. 8:28). This gives us confidence in the divinely managed outcomes in our times of distress.

We have the certain hope that He will justly care for our enemies. This frees us from the burden of having to get back in revenge and releases us to love our enemies in return (1 Peter 2:20–23).

We have the certain hope that He is coming again. As He said to His disciples, "Let not your hearts be troubled. . . . If I go and prepare a place for you, I will come again and will take you to myself, that where I am you may be also" (John 14:1–3).

And those of us who have placed our hope in His return are motivated to purify ourselves in preparation for that time. As John says, "We know that when he appears we shall be like him, because we shall see him as he is. And everyone who thus hopes in him purifies himself as he is pure" (1 John 3:2–3).

For early Christians living under the oppressive reign of Rome, their unwavering hope in realities like these and many other promises triggered lives of optimism. They believed what God had said and what Jesus had taught and that in the end God would be faithful to all He had promised. No wonder that the writer to the Hebrews encouraged them to "hold fast the confession of our hope without wavering, for he who promised is faithful" (Heb. 10:23).

Neither is it any wonder that we sing the classic hymn "Great Is Thy Faithfulness" with its stirring words: "Strength for today and bright hope for tomorrow, blessings all mine and ten thousand beside. Great is thy faithfulness, morning by morning new mercies I see; all I have needed Thy hand has provided: great is thy faithfulness, Lord, unto me."[18]

Early Christians' optimism was found in the fact that they had "strength for today and bright hope for tomorrow" in the promises of their faithful God.

LIVING HOPE IN ACTION

Steve Cochlan, a friend of mine, was recently diagnosed with ALS, commonly known as Lou Gehrig's disease. If there is a list of ailments nobody wants to die from, ALS is at the top. The disease slowly disintegrates the functionality of all of your muscles so that you get to the point that you can't swallow, breathe, or carry out your basic functions of survival. Getting news from the doctor that you are a victim of ALS would understandably trigger deep hopelessness in even the best of us.

Yet I have watched Steve go through the ordeal with a surprising sense of joy and hope. It's no doubt attributable to God's sustaining grace and to Steve's willingness to place his hope in his Lord and His promises. He continually reminds me that he wants to be sure that God gets the glory through this season of his life.

Steve decided to get busy and make something of his bad news. In the midst of his own trouble, he wondered if he could find a way to share the love of Jesus with others who had the same disease. He and his team started a ministry called the ALS Family of Faith, which offers "Christ-centered love and support at no cost to the recipients." Tanya Hageman, care services coordinator, explains, "We are currently serving approximately 100 people, but throughout the past three years we have been able to serve over 300 people and have had over 5,000 sessions with people in this community. Our numbers fluctuate so often because people are dying so quickly from this disease. Because we pair ALS patients, their loved ones, and caregivers with a care partner who can meet with them on a regular basis, we are unique, as there is no other organization that pairs people with the same person to meet with on a regular basis."[19]

I asked Steve to send me a video of his testimony that I could use in a series that I was doing on the biblical concept of joy. He closed his testimony speaking of the importance of joy, thanksgiving, and hope. The joy and thanksgiving that according to Paul fit the profile of a kingdom person in the midst of trouble (Col. 1:11–12). He said, "There are days when I get down, but you know what? God calls us to be joyful and to give thanks in all circumstances. He wants us to have fellowship with Him, and that's the only way we can be thankful and have a hope for all of eternity that when we get to heaven we will be partying with other believers, friends, and families. So, get out there and kick some tail for Jesus and love everyone you come into contact with. Everyone! And don't waste a day!"

. . . .

There is little doubt that the most significant driver of this faith-based optimism for the early church, for Steve, and for the rest of us is the promise of His return and our eternal fellowship with Him.

A friend of mine founded a home for children with cognitive disabilities. Despite their challenges, some were able to understand the gospel and would accept Christ as their Savior. I remember my friend asking me, "Joe, do you know what our biggest housekeeping challenge is?"

Of course, I had no clue, so he said, "Dirty windows!"

When I replied, "Dirty windows?" he told me that these hopeful children would often go to the windows and press their faces and hands to the glass looking to the sky to see if this was the day that Jesus was coming for them.

In my dad's last days, we would sing some of his favorite songs by his bedside. He especially liked, "Sing the wondrous love of Jesus, sing His mercy and His grace; in the mansions bright and blessed, He'll prepare for us a place. When we all get to heaven, what a day of rejoicing that will be! When we all see Jesus, we'll sing and shout the victory!"[20]

Who wouldn't be optimistic with a hope like this!

TO THINK ABOUT

When you feel a surge of hopelessness, what certainties can you cling to that reinvigorate your heart? Name them. Would you say that those you live and work with would think of you as a hopeful person?

SIX

WHAT'S LOVE GOT TO DO WITH IT?

. . . .

The greatest of these is love.

1 CORINTHIANS 13:13

I t's hard to escape the reality that "love" is at the core of the kingdom mission of Jesus. God's love for the world was the impetus for sending Jesus in the first place (John 3:16). Jesus showed the greatest kind of love by laying down His life for us (John 15:13).

Love is the leading theme of the two "greatest commandments," as Jesus said, "You shall love the Lord your God with all your heart and with all your soul and with all your mind. . . . And a second is like it: You shall love your neighbor as yourself" (Matt. 22:37–39).

Paul tells us that God loves us with a love that is so certain that "neither death nor life, nor angels nor rulers, nor things present not things to come, nor powers, nor height nor depth, nor anything else in creation, will be able to separate us from the love of God in Christ Jesus our Lord" (Rom. 8:37–39). If you think of all the high-level virtues that Scripture affirms, Paul reminds us that "the greatest of these is love" (1 Cor. 13:13). This is no doubt why James called love the "royal law" (James 2:8).

But watching many of us navigate our non-Jesus world, love would not be near the top of our behavioral attributes. For some of us, it would seem too soft, too ineffective in defeating the enemy. Yet it is love that may just be the most powerful weapon we have in dissolving the chill of cultural critics and attracting others to Christ.

This is why Jesus calls us to love in four different relational contexts. We are to love our God. We are to love our neighbors. We are to love our enemies. And we are to love one another. All four of these life habits play a significant role in influencing our world for Christ.

THERE'S LOVE . . . AND THERE'S LOVE

We may be somewhat confused about the primacy of love since our culture has both redefined and distorted the meaning of love. The cultural thought of love has been individualized and sexualized. Both are illegitimate perceptions of true love. No doubt that legitimate sexual relationships are an expression of love, but today's permissive society thinks of love sexually far beyond the bounds of legitimacy. And, given our addiction to self, self-love is a hot topic today. However, since true love is about giving to and caring for others, self-love, in a sense, is a contradiction. In fact, an appropriate understanding of biblical love brings us to the conclusion that the opposite of love is not hate but self-centeredness.

Thankfully Jesus came to clarify what true love, pure love, is like.

When the commands of Jesus to "love" are recorded, the Greek word used for love is *agape*. As you are probably aware, the Greeks had several words for love. *Eros* was the word for sexual love. *Philos* was their word of familial love, as in how you feel about your brothers and sisters . . . maybe after you're twenty-five, LOL! But *agape* love stands apart as a unique kind of relational asset.

Agape is a love that cares for others and actualizes its energy to meet the needs of others. It is not a response to someone else's love for us. It loves regardless. It's most often used of the kind of love that God has for us. Is there anyone reading this book who is thankful that God loves you regardless? *Agape* love is not driven by how I feel. It is a choice to help meet others' needs whether I feel like it or not.

You don't necessarily have to like someone to *agape* them. I'm quite sure that there are times that God doesn't especially like things that I do. But I'm confident that He continues to care for me and seeks faithfully to meet my needs. Thankfully God's *agape* love extends even to His enemies. As Paul reminds us, "God shows his love for us in that while we were still sinners, Christ died for us. . . . For if while we were enemies we were reconciled to God by the death of his Son, much more, now that we are reconciled, shall we be saved by his life" (Rom. 5:8–10). It should not be missed that God's signature title in the Old Testament, what He is mostly known for, is as a God of "steadfast love and faithfulness." In the book of Psalms, God's "steadfast love" is noted 127 times, and in twenty-five of those, it is connected to His faithfulness.

Agape love is this kind of love that we are called to as citizens of the kingdom. Kingdom love cares. It meets needs. Toward everyone. Even when we may not feel like it or like everything about the recipients of our love. And it is inclusive of those we may see as our enemies. It is an attitude that proves its sincerity in helping and healing actions. The dynamics of this kind of love are affirmed in a passage as elementary as John 3:16. God loves the world, even—or especially—a world and its systems that are under the spell of darkness. It's a world that is at enmity with Him and in great need of restoration and redemption. But in spite of all of that, His love compels Him to reach past the offense of this world and give His most valuable resource to meet that need: His Son. And whoever embraces the gift of His Son will not perish but be redeemed and restored, and they will have everlasting life. That's the transforming power of love! The kind of love we take into our increasingly dark world. And, at the risk of using a word that has been trivialized, this is truly awesome.

LOVING GOD

The religious leaders of Christ's day were constantly trying to embarrass Christ in public by asking Him questions, hoping He'd give a wrong answer that would disenfranchise Him from the masses who followed Him. On one occasion they sent one of their lawyers to ask Christ a question. The conversation went like this: "But when the Pharisees heard that he had silenced the Sadducees, they gathered together. And one of them, a lawyer, asked him a question to test him. 'Teacher, which is the great commandment in the Law?'" (Matt. 22:34–36).

It's interesting that fellow Pharisees chose their lawyer to ask the question. There was a reason. A rough count of the laws in the Torah has commonly been 613. But the Pharisees had expanded the laws of righteous behavior to the unbelievable number of about 1,500. What had started out as civic, moral, and ceremonial rules for Israel became a massive and complex system of conformity to the ways of Judaism. For example, to the commandment to not work on the Sabbath, the Pharisees added lists of what all was prohibited, down to swatting a fly. It was so complicated that they needed Pharisees who were legal experts to adjudicate the complexities. Given the long list, any answer that Jesus might give would be grounds for a debate with the lawyer who knew the intricacies of the law better than anyone else. The goal was to discredit Jesus as a legitimate teacher of the law.

You've got to love the way Jesus in His wisdom (Col. 2:3) responds in situations like this. On this occasion, He dug deep into the Old Testament where we find Moses citing the ultimate requirement of the law which was, "Hear O Israel, the LORD our God, the LORD is one. You shall love the LORD your God with all your heart and with all your soul and with all your might" (Deut. 6:4–5). So that's how Christ answered: "You shall love the Lord your God with all your heart and with all your soul and with all your mind" (Matt. 22:37). No argument here. They would have had to agree that this was the pinnacle expression of loyalty to God. Clearly there are many ways to show our love and loyalty to God. We show our love for God in this non-Jesus world when we put Him first in all aspects of our lives. When we are not ashamed to be called His followers. When we choose to spend time with Him in His Word and commune with Him in prayer. But the pinnacle proof of our love for Him is obedience to Him.

When Jesus affirmed this as the greatest of all the commands in the Old Testament, He recognized its continuity into New Testament living as well. What then does loving God mean for us, particularly in our quest to find out "How should we then live?" In Jesus' last words to His disciples, He explains that when we obey God we abide in His love (John 15:9–10). So obedience is the evidence of our love—not just singing about how we love Him or even telling

> *Obedience is the evidence of our love, and obedience to Him is measured by how we treat other people.*

Him in prayer that we do. He wants to know if we are obedient in our attitudes and actions because that is where and when He feels loved by us. It is His love language.

We don't always like doing everything His way. We like control, not being controlled. We like living in the ways that seem right to us, ways that are more comfortable. More seemingly satisfying. But in the end, we need to remember that His ways are always better ways. Our ways are the ways that end in, as Proverbs 14:12 tells us, death!

When our children were young, we lived in a neighborhood where the older boys played ball in the street. When my little five-year-old wanted to go and play with them, I told him that because I loved him he couldn't play there. I didn't want his little body integrated into the grill of a Mack Truck. It's like that with God's interest in our obedience. He knows where Satan's traffic is. And it is because He loves us and wants the best for us that He welcomes us to obey.

Best of all, obeying Him puts us in the power lane of influencing our world according to the ways and will of Jesus. And three of those acts of obedience are particularly important to dissolving the hostility and attracting others to the cross. Those three are: to love our neighbor, to love our enemies, and to love one another.

To answer the question of how we should live in this world gone wrong, we must obediently follow His ways and His will as we seek to bring His light to the darkness. This is an act of love to Him. And He calls us to show our love for Him by loving our neighbor as much as we love ourselves.

LOVING OUR NEIGHBOR

Jesus adds a second commandment in answer to the Pharisee's question. "[Loving God] is the great and first commandment. And a second is like it: You shall love your neighbor as yourself" (Matt. 22:37–39). This is a direct quote from Leviticus 19:18, where an instruction of how to treat others is found. While the questioners hadn't asked for a two-fold answer, He couldn't separate the two commandments because they are theologically and logically inseparable.

Since loving God is obeying Him, then obedience to Him is measured by how we treat other people. In other words, you can't say you love God if you don't treat people well. Then, remarkably, He added, "On these two commandments depend all the Law and the Prophets" (Matt. 22:40). He just reduced the burden of multiple commands to two, which, when you think of it, makes sense. If you love your neighbor, you don't lie to them, you don't cheat them, you don't slander them, you don't sleep with their spouse, you don't covet what they have, you don't take out revenge against them . . . and the list goes on!

The attorney would have agreed that loving your neighbor is biblically important, since he would have known the Leviticus passage. But the enduring question among Jews was, "Who is my neighbor?" This is why on another occasion a lawyer quizzed Jesus with that question (Luke 10:29). In reply, Jesus told the story of the Good Samaritan, which had to be shocking to the Pharisee who would have considered a Samaritan to be the enemy, not the hero. Samaritans and Jews were at religious and political loggerheads with a long history of animosity between the two factions. But as Jesus told the tale, it was the unlikely guy from the other side, not the religious elites who were passing by, who sacrificially loved his neighbor. His neighbor was a Jew, one of those "other kinds of people," beaten and left to die by the side of the road. Christ's answer highlights a wide swath of candidates who are qualified to be recipients of our love.

Every day there are opportunities to show our love to someone else as an expression of our love for God and the betterment of their lives.

In fact, the word used in Scripture for neighbor does not just mean the folks next door. It encompasses all those who cross our path.

Let's say that Martie calls and asks me to pick up a salad on my way home from work because supper is almost ready. I rush into the store and, with the salad in hand, head to the express checkout, the lane that was designated "fifteen items or less." The person in front of me is unloading twenty-one items onto the checkout belt. If you wonder how I knew it was twenty-one items, I counted them! That person is my neighbor. I'm not sure how to love them . . . maybe I could ask if I could bag the groceries for him. At the least, I can avoid grousing or glaring at him. I might even smile and wish him a good day.

But more seriously, every day there are opportunities to show our love to someone else as an expression of our love for God and the betterment of their lives. It may not seem to make a difference on a large scale in regard to impacting our culture for Christ but daily, routine faithfulness on this front enables us to be in action when a significant opportunity does arise.

As I was leaving for my early morning run, Martie asked me to bring home a couple of lattes from Starbucks. So, with my run behind me, I walked into the Starbucks that had just opened. The guy in front of me had a copy of *The New York Times* he wanted to purchase—at that time Starbucks was still selling newspapers—and verbally abusing the barista for not having enough change for his fifty-dollar bill. He was brutal. Feeling sorry for the kid by the cash register, I said, "No worries, I'll pay for his paper." The customer was shocked, and on his way out turned and thanked me by saying, "All I have is yours!" Which obviously didn't include the fifty-dollar bill. Then, as I stepped up to place my order, the barista said, "Sir, that was a really nice thing you did. Our world would be a lot better place if there were more people like you!"

I knew that it was a chance to say something that would be a testimony, a moment of influence, but nothing came to mind, so I just made some self-deprecating remark and thanked him for the lattes. As I walked down the street, I was trying to think of what I could have said. And then it came to me. I should have said, "Well, the world wouldn't be a better place if more people were like me, but it would be a better place if more people were like Jesus because He taught me how to do these kinds of things." So I turned to go back to say that to the barista, only to find that there was now a long line and it didn't seem like a good idea to break into the line with a religious speech. As I resumed my journey home, I realized that I was wearing my old beat-up Moody Bible Institute cap. I thought, *I hope he saw the hat and knew that the world would be a better place because Jesus people do these kinds of things.*

Neighbors are everywhere, which means that there are golden opportunities every day to practice this influential habit. In fact, let's agree to commit an act of neighborly love once a day just to stay in shape!

LOVING OUR ENEMIES

In His teaching on kingdom values and behavior in the Sermon on the Mount, Jesus told His followers, "You have heard it said, 'You shall love your neighbor and hate your enemy.' But I say to you, Love your enemies and pray for those who persecute you, so that you may be sons of your Father who is in heaven" (Matt. 5:43–45). Loving your neighbor and hating your enemy was street talk. Kind of like, "I don't get mad, I just get even." But right-side-up followers don't get mad or even but rather seek to figure out ways to bless our enemies.

It always takes two to fight. Followers of Jesus leave their enemies shadowboxing by themselves.

Paul picked up this theme in Romans 12 when he wrote to persecuted Christians,

> Repay no one evil for evil, but give thought to do what is honorable in the sight of all. If possible, so far as it depends on you, live peaceably with all. Beloved, never avenge yourselves, but leave it to the wrath of God, for it is written, "Vengeance is mine, I will repay, says the Lord." To the contrary, "if your enemy is hungry feed him; if he is thirsty give him something to drink; for by so doing you will heap burning coals on his head." Do not be overcome by evil, but overcome evil with good. (Rom. 12:17–21)

One thing is liberatingly clear in this text. Getting back at our enemies is God's responsibility. It is not ours. Loving them is our business. It always takes two to fight. Followers of Jesus leave their enemies shadowboxing by themselves.

So the question remains for kingdom people, "What does it mean for me to love my enemy?"

It's easier to think what it doesn't mean. Loving my enemy doesn't mean that I slander and gossip about them, hoping to rally others to join my vendetta against them. It doesn't mean that I plot for ways to get back at them. It doesn't mean that I revile them and cast verbal stones at them. It doesn't mean that I mock them and belittle them with names and verbal disdain. It doesn't mean that I refuse to forgive them.

So what *do* we do? Luke helps us categorize ways in which we can love our enemies. When he records Christ's words in the Sermon on the Mount, he specifically states that Christ said, "*Do good* to those who hate you, *bless* those who curse you, *pray* for those who abuse you" (Luke 6:27–28). In Luke's terms, these three things qualify as acts of love to those who oppose us.

Do Good to My Enemy

Paul fills in this blank by saying if your enemy is hungry, feed him. If he is thirsty, give him something to drink (see Rom. 12:20). Sensing the needs of an enemy and then filling that need is a loving thing to do.

Several years ago, Dan Cathy, then CEO of Chick-fil-A, had made statements affirming the biblical stance on same-sex marriage as his personal opinion: nothing about employing or serving those who disagree. A coalition of gay advocates decided to boycott Chick-fil-A establishments to protest his viewpoint. Mr. Cathy, in a kingdom response, turned the tables by instructing his employees to take chicken sandwiches out to those picketing their stores! Brilliant!

He then called the leader of the boycott initiative and asked if he could stop by his office and meet with him. No doubt the leader of the boycott thought he'd be getting into an angry confrontation from Cathy, but just the opposite took place. Cathy said he wanted to get to know him, and from that initial conversation, he and Cathy started up a lasting friendship.

Though Dan Cathy later said he regretted that the company unwittingly and unfairly became affiliated as "anti-gay,"[21] we can still look to his gracious example as one to emulate. It's possible that through his actions of grace, the activist's heart is more open to the message of Jesus than if Dan had put on the gloves and threatened to take the activist to court over the depreciation of his business.

Bless My Enemy

This means that we pivot from vengeful attitudes to thinking of positive ways that we can bring benefit to their lives. This will take the shape of many different responses depending on the circumstances. And while it will often be challenging to think of ways to do this, prayerfully posturing ourselves to be ready to respond when the opportunity arises is important. Think of being the first one to bring food to the family of an adversary when they are in a health crisis; of sending a note of condolence in a time of loss; of apologizing for any part you may have played in the demise of your relationship; or of speaking well of them when others try to team up against them.

One of the most important steps that followers of Jesus take to bless our offenders is to step into their lives with the gift of forgiveness.

The importance of this is clear. In His Sermon on the Mount, Jesus says, "If you forgive others their trespasses, your heavenly Father will also forgive you. But if you do not forgive others their trespasses, neither will your Father forgive your trespasses" (Matt. 6:14–15).

Forgiveness is highly important to God because in Scripture forgiveness is transactional. Since we have been given the gift of forgiveness, we are to pass that gift on to others. When we are unwilling to be like Him by refusing to forgive others, in His view, this is a serious problem.

THIS LIGHT OF MINE

Peter, perhaps trying to impress Jesus, asked how many times he should forgive someone who sinned against him. "As many as *seven times?*" Jesus suggested it would be more like seventy-seven times. Jesus went on to tell the parable of a servant who owed his master a large debt that he could not pay. When the master decided to sell him and his family into slavery, the servant pled for mercy, and Jesus said,

> Out of pity for him, the master of that servant released him and forgave him the debt. But when that same servant went out, he found one of his fellow servants who owed him a hundred denarii and seizing him, he began to choke him, saying, "Pay what you owe." So his fellow servant fell down and pleaded with him, "Have patience with me, and I will pay you." He refused and went and put him in prison until he should pay the debt. When his fellow servants saw what had taken place, they were greatly distressed, and they went and reported to their master all that had taken place. Then his master summoned him and said to him, "You wicked servant! I forgave you all that debt because you pleaded with me. And should not you have had mercy on your fellow servant, as I had mercy on you?" And in anger his master delivered him to the jailers, until he should pay all his debt. So also my heavenly Father will do to every one of you, if you do not forgive your brother from your heart. (Matt. 18:27–35)

When thinking of forgiving an offender it is important to remember that we have been forgiven at the cost of His shed blood. And since we have been forgiven to that extent, it is unreasonable to think that we shouldn't dispense forgiveness to others even when it seems costly to us.

There are a lot of reasons why we might think that blessing our enemies with forgiveness is a bad idea.

They don't deserve my forgiveness! That is true. But we don't forgive because they deserve it, we forgive because we have been forgiven and forgiving is what followers do. Forgiveness has nothing to do with our offender and everything to do with my obedient love for God as a recognition of His amazing gift of forgiveness for me.

I can't forget what they have done. While we are often told to forgive and forget, forgetting is impossible. The only one who can forget is God who separates our offense to Him as far as the east is from the west. But what we can do is to attach new meaning to our memories. New meaning that is anchored in the reality that God in His providence never wastes your sorrow and promises, that in time and in His ways all will be made right, and that in our suffering He is working to shape and mold us into His likeness. Reframing the memories sends us on a journey to look for the ways that His hand is at work in our lives to make us more like Jesus. And if you wonder if God can possibly overcome the evil done to you with good outcomes, then think of the cross. Jesus—Creator, Son of God—was cruelly slain in shame as a criminal, and by God's grace and power you and I today, as we read this, have had our hell canceled and our heaven secured as a result of the evil done to Him. God loves to turn the best efforts of Satan into our good and His glory (Rom. 8:28).

I'll forgive them when they ask for it! Forgiveness is an unconditional response. We can all be thankful that Christ forgave us long before we asked for it when He died on the cross for our sins. Since unforgiving attitudes have negative effects on our own lives, the sooner we unload the burden of bitterness and planned revenge the better for us.

> Forgiveness may be among the most challenging virtues for light bearers, particularly for those who have been deeply violated.

If I forgive them they will get away with bad behavior! They won't get away with it since God promises in the end to deal with our enemies. As He said, "Vengeance is mine, I will repay." In fact, if justice is your primary reason for not forgiving, let us remember that God is the dispenser of justice and in time

He will make all things right. Giving that responsibility to God frees us to look for opportunities to love our enemies (Luke 23:34).

In Victor Hugo's *Les Misérables*, Jean Valjean is imprisoned for nineteen years of hard labor after stealing bread for his sister's starving children. After his release, Valjean is unable to find work or a place of refuge for the night until he comes face to face with Bishop Myriel. The bishop feeds him and gives him a place to sleep. But, after a night of struggling with haunting thoughts of his past, Valjean steals the bishop's silverware and flees. Captured by the police, he is brought back to the bishop's home. Fearful of his fate, Valjean is shocked when the bishop tells the police that the silverware was a gift. Not only does the bishop return the silverware to Valjean but he hands him silver candlesticks as well. Stunned by grace, Valjean hears the bishop reminding him to reform his life because God has ransomed his soul.

I like to think that stunning our enemies with the grace of a loving and forgiving God may just open their ears to a call for repentance and a newly found life in Jesus. I recognize that forgiveness may be among the most challenging virtues for light bearers, particularly for those who have been deeply violated. I understand why it may be difficult to trigger forgiveness. My appeal here is to begin the journey into forgiveness by praying for a willing spirit to forgive. Again, not because our offender is deserving but because our highest desire in life is to honor Christ and forgive as we have been forgiven. Pray that your willing spirit will mature into acts of forgiveness that bless your enemy with the healing attributes of love and mercy.

Pray for My Enemy

In a shocking admonition to persecuted believers, Paul says that they were to pray for "all who are in high positions" (1 Tim. 2:2). Sometimes we feel that, due to their worldview and their actions, those in high positions such as elected office are our enemies. Praying for decision-makers in our nation can be a challenge.

Tim Walberg is a Republican congressman representing the fifth congressional district of Michigan. He is one of the leaders of a bipartisan prayer group that meets regularly on Capitol Hill. They pray for one another, regardless of party affiliation. They pray for our president and for wisdom as they deliberate in the House of Representatives. Tim tells me that recently one of their congressional colleagues who is not a Christian and who is on the progressive end of the political spectrum attended the prayer group. Upon leaving, they told Tim that they were deeply moved and greatly appreciated the support they felt as the group prayed for them. I can't help but think that Tim's colleague's feeling toward Christians is far different than it would have been if they had never personally experienced the love of the group's prayers for them.

On a more personal level, after a difficult relational experience, I knew that I had to practice what I preach and to pray for the one who had offended me. Someone asked me, "What do you pray for when you pray for this person?" I had to admit that the prayer was pretty generic at first. But over time, I knew that asking our Father to help the person grow in ways to reflect Jesus in their life would be important. And it is appropriate to pray for our Lord's redemptive and transformative work in the lives of our offenders. Interestingly, you may find that praying for your enemy will move your mind to think of the ways that you should treat others and to ask God to make you more sensitive to your own faults as you seek to grow in love and grace.

In a chaotic world that is filled with civil unrest and angry responses toward oppositional forces, peace-making, enemy-loving people stand out as unusually different. Attractively different. Loving our enemies makes a statement to all who are fighting against us. The statement is that we are kingdom people, and we seek to find ways to love and bless them, which is why Paul could say, "Do not be overcome with evil, but overcome evil with good" (Rom. 12:21). And it shouldn't go unnoticed that Jesus shows us the way. When Peter, the militant, warred against the enemies of Christ by slicing off the ear of the servant of the high priest, Jesus said to Peter, "No more of this." And in a dramatic demonstration of kingdom love, He healed the wound of His enemy (Luke 22:50–51).

LOVING ONE ANOTHER

When Jesus chose His inner circle of followers, He found a challenging and diverse group of individuals. Some were in the trades as fishermen; there was the tax collector Matthew and the politically active Simon among others. They were unique in their personalities. Thomas was the skeptic. Peter was always the first one to speak up, at times even annoyingly verbal and impulsive. John was gentle yet emotionally explosive. They were at odds politically. Simon the Zealot was an anti-Roman revolutionary, hence his nickname. Matthew was an employee of Rome's revenue service.

The fact that they all managed to stay together in a meaningful cohort of followers was amazing, and attributable to one reality. In all of their differences, they shared one thing in common—Jesus. Allegiance to Him was their mutual priority. He was the glue and the reason for their being together. So it is easy to understand that Jesus was concerned about what would happen to their togetherness once He was gone. After all, He was trusting the future of His kingdom on earth to them. If they started fighting, dividing, and competing for position and power, the whole enterprise would be at risk.

His strategy for their ongoing togetherness? It is that they would love one another as He had loved them. Their mutual love would bond them together in spite of their differences and be a testimony to the watching world that they were His disciples. In one of Christ's last moments with them, just before His crucifixion, John records that He said, "Yet a little time I am with you. . . . Where I am going you cannot come. A new commandment I give you, that you love one another: just as I have loved you, you also are to love one another. By this all people will know that you are my disciples, if you have love for one another" (John 13:33–35).

The pattern for this bonding love was to be the way Jesus had loved them. And He did love them in spite of their differences. They were all recipients of Jesus' generous love, and now they were tasked with sharing that same kind of generous love with each other and with those

Unfortunately, instead of bringing Jesus into our fellowship as the center of all that we are and do, we have the propensity to bring cultural issues and personal preferences into our church world.

who would believe in Jesus. In a world highly bifurcated by personality and societal divisions, their unusual unity would be a testimony to the uniqueness of their lives as followers of Christ.

And thankfully it worked! They stayed together and took their world by storm for Christ and His kingdom.

Unfortunately, we have failed to follow their example. Instead of bringing Jesus into our fellowship as the center of all that we are and do, we have the propensity to bring cultural issues and personal preferences into our church world. It is no secret that our nation has been in an unusually challenging season for several years. Whether the issue was the Covid vaccination or how to respond to racial unrest; choosing which candidates to support; what position to take on aid that goes overseas; being influenced by conspiracy theories; and unfortunately pastors have been caught in the crossfire . . . we've had no end of issues that would divide us.

When we care more about our personal preferences and political and social views than we do about the worth and welfare of each other as brothers and sisters, we have shamed His name and misrepresented the heart of Jesus. But when we all rally around the primacy of Jesus as our reason for being together, and when we prove that our love for Jesus and our love for one another transcends all earthly differences, we send a resounding message to a watching world that there is something unique and special about the community of belief.

It shouldn't go unnoticed that early Christians did this so well that the word on the street was, "See how they love one another!" In a world of chaos, divisiveness, racial tensions, and cultural warfare, how wonderful it would be if we amazed our world with the fact that in spite of our differences, we love each other! That the fellowship of believers is a safe place to be where peace and love prevail. A mutual love that reflects Jesus' observation, "By this all people will know that you are my disciples, if you have love for one another" (John 13:35).

TO THINK ABOUT

How would you rate yourself in regard to your love for God given what you have learned from this chapter? Your love for your neighbor? Your love for your enemies? Your love for your brothers and sisters . . . even those who are annoyingly different? What will you do to improve your score?

SEVEN

DEALING WITH
THE DARKNESS

. . . .

*"Let your light shine before others, so that they may see your
good works and give glory to your Father who is in heaven."*

MATTHEW 5:16

When we were raising our children, we always told them that a good attitude was an important virtue in life. To reinforce the thought, we would often say "spirit check" when their attitudes began to slip.

My observation is that the church of Jesus Christ needs a "spirit check" in order to offer our watching world an attractive alternative. Think of our world watching us and noting that we are a people who, in spite of cultural pressure, persevere with joy and thanksgiving (Col. 1:9). What if they would see us as people who are confident, courageous, and compassionate and who interact with hopeful and loving attitudes? No doubt that would catch the attention of a world that would expect us to feel like despairing losers, given the marginalization and sometimes cancellation that is heaped on us.

And, considering the sense of despair that many feel given the angry divisiveness of our culture and the rising rates of suicide, anxiety, and general lack of happiness, it could just be that our positive attitudes will raise their curiosity as to why we are the way we are.

But as important as attitudes are, if we are to live like Jesus in a non-Jesus world, actions carry equal weight in lighting up the darkness of our culture.

In a letter written to persecuted Christians on how to navigate life "Jesus-ly," Peter underscores the importance of action when he writes: "Keep your conduct among the Gentiles honorable, so that when they speak against you as evildoers, they may see your good deeds and glorify God on the day of visitation" (1 Peter 2:12).

Honorable behavior is obviously a key to attracting the attention of those without Christ. This takes us back to what we discussed earlier in the book. While the world is no longer interested in what we have to say, they are still watching our attitudes and actions. Poor attitudes and hostility toward others are less than honorable behaviors. Having an attitude and behavior check is an important first step in initiating the strategy. But staying honorable is not always easy. When the world misrepresents us and maligns Christ followers as haters, it is easy to respond in less than honorable ways.

If you haven't noticed, we are often cast as the bad guys. We are the only subculture that is not protected by the "Political Correctness" cops. We can be portrayed as the stupid ones in sitcoms, made fun of by comedians, maligned for our stands on moral issues, and can be called names like hateful, intolerant, arrogant, and a host of other barbs that are verbally thrown at us. We understand what it means to be spoken of falsely.

WRONGLY ACCUSED

Early Christians were in the same situation yet took Peter's strategic advice seriously. They knew what it was like to be called the evil ones in their society. They were falsely accused of being cannibals in their gatherings as they "ate flesh and drank blood" at their Communion services. The word on the street was that they had orgies at these gatherings because they called their Communion dinners love feasts. They were derided as atheists since they only had one God and rejected the societal norm of a multiplicity of gods. They were called insurrectionists because they refused to chant with the crowds, "Caesar is Lord!" Their response, Peter says, should be to live honorably and be known among the Gentiles for their good works.

I think it's interesting that Peter goes on to say that living honorably means honoring all of the rulers over us. "Be subject for the Lord's sake to every human institution. . . . Honor everyone. Love the brotherhood. Fear God. Honor the emperor" (1 Peter 2:13, 17). This is radical kingdom obedience, especially since it was the emperor who often initiated the persecution.

Peter didn't come up with this strategy on his own. Matthew records Jesus' words to His disciples when He was preparing them for life in a hostile world. Jesus said, "Blessed are you when others revile you and persecute you and utter all kinds of evil against you falsely on my account" (Matt. 5:11). He then went on to tell them that in spite of the violent opposition, they were to be like what salt is to a good meal and what light is to the prevailing darkness (vv. 13–16). And it's the "light'" part that Jesus expands, detailing its influence on darkness. He says, "Let your light shine before others, so they may see your good works and give glory to your Father who is in heaven."

LIGHTING THE NIGHT

What does it mean for us to shine our lights into the darkness of our world? His "light the night" strategy has several key points.

First, we must assume that we live in darkness. I have often wondered why we are so shocked and disappointed that we live in a time when there is mounting opposition to us. The history of the church tells us that most Christians through the last two millennia have lived in hostile contexts. Many of our brothers and sisters around the world endure hardship daily, as reported by ministries that make the world aware of their plight and offer practical help. Some believers are imprisoned, some cannot find jobs, others have their homes or churches set on fire. And some even give the ultimate sacrifice. As of the time of this writing, the world had recently learned of the martyrdom in Haiti of American missionaries Davy and Natalie Lloyd and of Jude Montis, the local director of their mission agency. This mission's purpose is "to see the Gospel of Christ make a difference in the lives of Haiti's young people."[22]

> Shining the light is an activity. Light-shining is optical not verbal. It is for others to "see," not for others to hear.

We in the United States and other Western countries have easy lives compared to so many Christians in other parts of the globe. But just because we have had nearly 250 years of cultural consensus, relative ease, and blessings, there is no guarantee that we are entitled to a life of ease. The hymn writer Isaac Watts asks the right question when he writes, "Must I be carried to the skies on flow'ry beds of ease, while others fought to win the prize and sailed through bloody seas? Increase my courage Lord! I'll bear the toil, endure the pain, supported by Thy Word."[23] The darkness of our world is a given! The question is, how do we bring the light of Jesus to it?

Second, light-shining is an activity. We have talked about how our attitudes need to be attitudes that would attract and not detract from our kingdom message. But, as we have said, living like Jesus in a non-Jesus world is not just attitudinal, it is actional as well. The vast majority of Christ followers today have *not* responded like angry cultural warriors. But rather, assuming that we have lost and deciding that we can't do much about it, we resign ourselves to living passively until Jesus comes. But Jesus challenges this passivity and asks us to actively assault the darkness with light—with the light of our good works.

Third, it is public. Carrying out this call to light the darkness is to be outward-bound. Lighting the night is about doing things out in the darkness. Actions that are observable to others. To others in our office, and in our neighborhoods, in traffic, at sporting events, at the airport check-in counter, and in stores . . . everywhere.

Fourth, light-shining is optical, not verbal. It is for others to "see," not for others to hear. For the most part, our world no longer wants to hear what we have to say. But it is clear they are still watching us, and maybe more closely than ever.

And, finally, the light is the power of our "good works."

So, in essence, Jesus is saying that as light dramatically influences darkness, we should be actively and publicly engaged in shedding the light of visible good works that catch the attention of a watching world.

THE POWER OF GOOD WORKS

What is this light of ours? It is our "good works." The Greeks had two words for "good": *agathos* means good behavior. It was used for law keeping and righteous living. A rule-keeper's favorite word. The other Greek word is *kalos*, which is the word for good in the sense of that which is beneficial, helpful, and caring. Jesus did not use *agathos* when it came to our efforts to reach out to a resistant world. Not that living righteously in light of God's commands isn't important. It is. Living righteously keeps our testimony credible so that we are not seen as hypocrites who say that we believe one thing is right and yet behave in the opposite way. Good behavior is a signature trait of followers of Jesus.

But in terms of drawing people to Christ, of lighting up the night, it's a nonstarter. Becoming a religious rule-keeper is not particularly appealing to a pagan. Try telling your unsaved friend that they should become a Christ follower because then they could tithe. Or go to church every week. Or stop sleeping around. On the contrary, in Jesus' mind, a life committed to the benefit and welfare of others is what will light up the world and attract others to Jesus.

It should not go unnoticed that throughout the ministry of Jesus He exhibited this "good works" kingdom strategy. As Matthew records, "He went throughout all Galilee, teaching in their synagogues and proclaiming the gospel of the kingdom and healing every disease and every affliction among the people" (Matt. 4:23). His fame was fanned by the fact that He cared for all, even the unclean, Samaritans, and other outsiders of the Jewish establishment, and that He offered to heal their afflictions.

This was *kalos* in divine skin. It's no wonder that "his fame spread throughout all Syria, and they brought him all the sick, those afflicted with various diseases and pains, those oppressed by demons, those having seizures, and paralytics, and he healed them. And great crowds followed him from Galilee and the Decapolis, and from Jerusalem and Judea, and from beyond the Jordan" (vv. 24–25).

Living like Jesus in our non-Jesus world means that we too must follow His example and fan the flame of the fame of His name by actively caring for others with good works that minister to their needs.

Agathos behaves . . . *kalos* blesses.

Agathos does what is right . . . *kalos* forgives those who don't.

Agathos goes to church . . . *kalos* takes church to the world

Agathos tithes . . . *kalos* gives above the tithe to those in need with no thought of receiving in return.

Agathos does not do what others at the office do . . . *kalos* keeps a keen eye out at the office for opportunities to express the love of Jesus to others.

Kalos lights up our world with attention-getting works that arouse curiosity. You can't be like Jesus in your non-Jesus world without *kalos*. It arouses a curiosity that may just open the door of people's hearts to hear about the one who has taught us to live a *kalos* life.[24]

Early Christians Lead the Way

The first Christians were living within the Roman Empire and, as we have seen, this situation presented them with some sobering challenges. However, the Roman Empire actually contributed to the spread of Christianity through their remarkable system of roads, comprising about 50,000 miles. While these were constructed primarily for military reasons to expand the Empire, good transportation and an era of relative peace eased the way for the good news about Jesus to spread, especially from city to city.

While no one can definitively state how many people were following Christ in the early centuries, many scholars have studied the issue. Sociologist and former Baylor University professor Rodney Stark is often cited as an authority on this question, and his estimate was a "global Christian population of 40,000 in AD 150." This number rose to about 100,000 around the year 180. By AD 200, it was 218,000, and by the year 250, it was likely up to 1.7 million.[25]

Jesus had directed His disciples to proclaim Him, beginning in Jerusalem, expanding to the surrounding regions, and finally throughout the world (Matt. 28:19–20; Luke 24:47; Acts 1:8). The movement grew quickly, stretching from Jerusalem to North Africa to Britain and all the way east to Turkey. No region of the Roman Empire was left untouched. By the fourth century, Emperor Constantine (AD 306–337) became a convert and, with the Edict of Milan in 313, permanently established tolerance for Christianity. Christians had legal rights, and property that had been confiscated during times of persecution was returned.[26] Constantine credited his political successes to his conversion to Christianity and to the support of God.[27]

Legalizing a religion and forbidding its adherents to be persecuted does not alone account for the spread of Christianity. Those who have studied the phenomena have generally agreed that it was due not so much to the tenets of the faith—though that certainly played a role—but to the lives of believers and the loving, even sacrificial works evident in their lives.

Even Emperor Julian (361–363), called the Apostate because he had been raised a Christian but later renounced the faith, wrote that Christianity "has been specially advanced through the loving service rendered to strangers . . . the godless Galilaeans care not only for their own poor, but ours [Romans] as well, while those who belong to us look in vain for the help that we should render them."[28] Christians then as now were obeying Jesus, who stated that whatever good works were done for others, it was actually ministry to Him (Matt. 25:35–36).

> To this day, two thousand years later, historians applaud the unprecedented kalos effect that early Christians had in their world.

In the second century, Saint Lawrence, a deacon in the early church and treasurer of the church's resources, was brought before the authorities and asked to hand over all the church's treasures to the government. To refuse meant certain death. He asked for eight days to gather the treasures of the church, at which time he promised to present them to the emperor's representative. On the eighth day, he appeared and brought with him orphans, the poor, the lame, and widows in distress. Pointing to them, he told the authorities, "These are the treasures of the church!" For that reply, Lawrence was martyred, roasted on a spit over burning coals.

Christians would often fast, not for their own gain or spiritual advantage, as we often do, but rather to take the money they would have spent on food and give it to the poor. The early church father Hermas wrote, "On the day when you fast, take only bread and wine. Calculate the amount of feed you would have taken on other days, put aside the money you would have spent on it and give to the widow, the orphan or the poor." Origen of Alexandria said, "Let the poor man be provided with food from the self-denial of him who fasts." Early bishops in the church were required to eat one meal each day with the poor.

To this day, two thousand years later, historians applaud the unprecedented *kalos* effect that early Christians had in their world.

Today, we deplore the tragedy of abortion. The Romans had their own form of ridding themselves of an unwanted child: exposure. Babies who were imperfect or even the wrong sex could be discarded as garbage and left to die. Christians would rescue these precious ones and care for them and raise them in their own homes. The prolific Christian author Tertullian (AD 160–200) is quoted as writing, "It is our care of the helpless, our practice of loving-kindness that brands us in the eyes of many of our opponents, who say, 'See those Christians, how they love one another.'"

Christians' response during two epic plagues further explains how Christianity grew in those early years. In 165, an epidemic known as the Plague of Galen lasted for fifteen years, ravaging the Empire and taking the lives of at least a quarter of the population. Then a century later another plague hit. As many as five thousand people died every day, and this was just in the city of Rome. Anyone who could, fled. Even in an age when little was understood of the origin of disease, the terrified people understood contagion well enough to know to put as much distance between themselves and the afflicted. During this plague, Bishop Dionysius of Alexandria wrote (ca. 251), "At the first onset of disease, [pagans] pushed the sufferers away and fled from their dearest, throwing them into the roads before they were dead and treated unburied corpses as dirt, hoping thereby to avert the spread and contagion of the fatal disease, but do what they might, they found it difficult to escape."[29]

Christians had a different response. Rather than flee, they stayed and nursed those who had fallen victim to disease. They provided basic needs of food, water, and sanitation, likely cutting the mortality rate by at least two-thirds, though their interaction and care for the afflicted also cost many Christians their lives. Again quoting Dionysius,

> Most of our brother Christians showed unbounded love and loyalty, never sparing themselves and thinking only of one another. Heedless of the danger, they took charge of the sick, attending to their every need and ministering to them in Christ, and with them departed this life serenely happy; for they were infected by others with the disease, drawing on themselves the sickness of their neighbors and cheerfully accepting their pains.

While the doctrines of the Christian faith are essential for us to understand and defend, the early Christians did more than preach. They rescued discarded babies on the trash pile, elevated the status of women, protected rather than abused children, provided for the poor, and dared to be close enough to those stricken with terrible disease to relieve their suffering and care for their practical needs. They were the hands and feet of Jesus. Their loving deeds brought the power of *kalos* to their world, melting resistance and opening hearts and minds to the good news of Jesus. It was the power of those good deeds that lit the night around them and ultimately drew thousands to join the ranks of this newly formed faith It was kingdom work at its best!

. . . .

Historian Will Durant, who was usually contemptuous toward Christianity, wrote this about the influence of early Christians on their culture:

> All in all, no more attractive religion has ever been presented to mankind. It offered itself without restrictions to all individuals, classes, and nations; it was not limited to one people, like Judaism, nor to the freemen of one

state, like the official cults of Greece and Rome. By making all men heirs of Christ's victory over death, Christianity announced the basic equality of men, and made transiently trivial all differences of earthly degree. To the miserable, maimed, bereaved, disheartened, and humiliated it brought the new virtue of compassion, and an ennobling dignity . . . it brightened their lives with the hope of the coming Kingdom, and of endless happiness beyond the grave. To even the greatest sinners, it promised forgiveness, and their full acceptance into the community of the saved. To minds harassed with the insoluble problems of origin and destiny, evil and suffering, it brought a system of divinely revealed doctrine in which the simplest soul could find mental rest . . . into a world sick of brutality, cruelty, oppression, and sexual chaos . . . it brought a new morality of brotherhood, kindliness, decency, and peace. So molded to men's wants, the new faith spread with fluid readiness. Nearly every convert, with the ardor of a revolutionary, made himself an office of propaganda.[30]

—————— TO THINK ABOUT ——————

Has your walk with Christ been more focused on the importance of agathos than the importance of a life characterized by kalos? Can you envision ways that you can ignite the light of a kalos activity in your life? Can you think of a time when the "good works" of your life caught the attention of the world you live in?

EIGHT

"THIS LIGHT OF MINE!"

. . . .

Let us consider how to stir up one
another to love and good works.

HEBREWS 10:24

M ost of us who grew up in the church world are familiar with the song we were taught in Sunday school about lighting up our world.[31] Its words were simple yet profoundly directive in terms of Jesus' strategy for living like Him in the darkness. Do you know it?

> This little light of mine, I'm going to let it shine! . . .
> Hide it under a bushel? No! I'm going to let it shine.
> All around the neighborhood, I'm going to let it shine.
> Let it shine till Jesus comes! I'm going to let it shine!

The good news is that—like the early Christians—churches and mission organizations and individuals are living out the words of that song, making significant progress toward melting the resistance to the gospel and leading many to Christ.

AND THE DARKNESS SHALL NOT OVERCOME IT

Beyond Church Walls

The church Martie and I attend, Crossroads Bible Church in Grand Rapids, actively contributes to the needs of our community through effective *kalos* programming. Led by our head pastor, Rod VanSolkema, the church relocated downtown to better serve the urban community. Given the needs of the neighborhood, including children who are mostly from impoverished single-parent homes, Crossroads placed a full-time staff member in a nearby school. The principal, needing help with the challenges of educating in this kind of environment, gave the staff member an office, so our staff member had a presence in the daily ongoing of the school. This staff member oversees programs specifically designed to meet the students' needs, often providing winter coats, boots, food, and other necessities that the children otherwise would not have.

In addition, volunteers from the church provide academic mentoring for the students and more importantly, share the love of Jesus to many who come from difficult homes. Some mentors stay with the same child throughout their elementary school journey, fostering lasting friendships. No doubt the children will always remember that it was Jesus' people who loved them like this, paving the way for them to open the door of their hearts to Christ.

The church also actively ministers to homeless individuals and families, offering weekly access to the church facilities for job assistance, counseling, medical advice, and essential supplies. Recently, a section of the church building was repurposed in order to provide showers and sleeping space. During a recent Sunday service, in an open mic testimony time, a gentleman shared his testimony about being homeless. He then expressed gratitude for finding Christ at our church, where he felt loved and cared for.

> *The Wall Street Journal* published a story about the challenges faced by midsized American cities due to the flood of border immigrants causing a surge in homelessness rates.[32] When the journalist inquired about who was helping solve the problem in Grand Rapids, he was sent to Crossroads, which led to Crossroads' *kalos* programs being featured in the article. It says a lot to a watching nation to read that many evangelical Christians are bringing solutions to mounting challenges facing our communities. When the world acknowledges Christians' compassionate acts of love through such programs, it not only advertises well for the kingdom but breaks down the resistance to our message.

New Life Centers

Mark Jobe is the president of Moody Bible Institute. After completing his education at Moody and Columbia International University, he began his ministry as a pastor of a small Latino church on the southwest side of Chicago. Having grown up as a missionary kid in Spain, he was fluent in Spanish and brought a heart to reach the Hispanic community of Chicago for Christ. Out of that small church, Mark, his wife, Dee, and their team began New Life Community Church, which now has twenty-seven locations holding over forty worship services in Chicagoland every Sunday as well as in eight cities in other countries. These congregations are in a variety of communities from upscale gentrified neighborhoods to first-generation immigrant neighborhoods. Worship services are held in four languages: English, Spanish, Mandarin, and Quiché.

After an encounter with a sixteen-year-old who had dropped out of high school and was involved in a gang, Mark felt compelled to start a church-based nonprofit organization, New Life Centers, which helps thousands of disadvantaged, often gang-affiliated and at-risk youth, in the city of Chicago. The Center has grown from one staff to over two hundred staff who influence thousands of youths for Christ in various neighborhoods of the city.

Under the leadership of director Matt DeMateo, also a Moody graduate, New Life Centers is now mentoring youth through sports programs, after school tutoring, job training programs, and street intervention initiatives. During the pandemic, New Life Centers and New Life Church mobilized to help people caught in a food shortage. At the height of the pandemic, they were feeding 30,000 people a week in some of the hardest hit neighborhoods in Chicago. A partnership with the Chicago Food Depository helped them feed over three million people during the pandemic and become one of the largest food distributors in the state of Illinois. The impact was so significant that the mayor of Chicago dropped by multiple times to lend support.

More recently, when buses full of immigrants started coming from Texas, the city didn't have the capacity to assimilate the 40,000 that were dropped off. New Life Churches and Centers worked with the city and other groups to create a strategy to meet the buses, register the families, and help them find lodging and food. As a result, many immigrants have not only found hope but also faith in Christ. This has created many memorable scenes of shared meals, baptisms, weddings, and child dedications.

Making the World a Better Place

Ask the mayor or anyone else who has been watching, they would tell you Chicago is a better place because Christians are busy about the work of Jesus. And more wonderfully, heaven will be bursting at the seams with some from several tribes and nations who were loved by this church and others working for the kingdom. And not because they first of all heard the messages of the pastors but because they first of all felt the love of Jesus through ordinary Christians on a mission to love and serve in His name.

On one camping trip, Martie and I met a couple from upstate Michigan. I told them I knew Scott Distler, who is a pastor in their town. When I told them the name of the church they immediately replied, "Oh yes, that's a great church. They do a lot to make our community a better place. In fact, when a recent tornado went through, they headquartered the relief and recovery work." My guess is that that church has an open door to tell people in that town that Jesus is the one who has taught them to do these kinds of things.

Volumes could be written about the thousands of churches throughout America that are quietly but effectively programming the love of Jesus to the needy and the lost. It is a slow process, not a weekend evangelistic crusade in the local stadium, but it is a good process. It's the strategy that Jesus set in motion when He welcomed us to His kingdom and told us that in His kingdom, *kalos* light-bearers are the front lines of the gospel in a dark and needy world.

> As kalos *work usually does, it gives credibility to the message of hope that the churches proclaim.*

I serve on the board of International Aid, a relief ministry headed by my friend J. C. Huizenga. I'm thankful for opportunities like this to invest my time, talents, and treasures with a ministry that takes relief to needy people in the name of Jesus. Among the many good things this excellent organization does, I especially like that they work with local churches in the distribution of aid. This puts the churches in the spotlight as a local, caring solution to the needs of crisis-ridden people. And, as *kalos* work usually does, it gives credibility to the message of hope that the churches proclaim and opens the hearts of the recipients to the good news of Jesus' redemptive gift of salvation.

I also serve on the board of CURE International alongside their president, Justin Narducci. CURE is a medical mission agency operating seven hospitals in Africa and the (Tim) Tebow CURE Hospital in the Philippines. CURE brings the love of Christ to children who have severe birth deformities such as clubfeet, bowed legs, cleft lips and cleft palate, severe burn injuries, spina bifida, and hydrocephalus. These children often come from remote villages where their disabilities have marginalized them and their families since many of the villagers think that their deformity is because of a curse or bad omen to the family.

Often these children are abandoned by their fathers and shunned by other children. They come to our hospitals where they are surprised by the loving reception and services they receive after being ostracized at home and in their communities. The surgeries are at no cost to the families since many come from impoverished backgrounds. Each hospital has a spiritual team who shares the gospel with the patient and their families. Through this, many express their faith in Christ, and when they return to their villages healed and able to function normally again, the villagers hear that the followers of Jesus at the hospital they visited showed them love and healed their infirmity. This is kingdom work at its best. As a result of the work of CURE, the name of Jesus is elevated in the villages as many more come to the saving knowledge of Christ and God is glorified.

To the Hard Places

Woodmen Valley Chapel, a church in Colorado Springs, is one of the churches in a network of evangelical churches in the Springs that band together to *kalos* the needs of their community. Under the banner of COS I LOVE YOU, they mutually take on projects that bring the love of Jesus to the needs of their city.

In the same spirit, under the leadership of Josh Lindstrom, lead pastor of teaching and vision, Woodmen Valley Chapel has a flourishing ministry to prisoners at the Ark Valley Correctional Facility. In fact, they count it to be their fifth campus. It's a ministry that strives toward positive change and rehabilitation within the criminal justice system, guided by the principles of faith, redemption, and genuine presence. Leading the ministry is campus pastor Howie Close, who connects well with the prisoners, having been incarcerated himself in the Colorado Department of Corrections for twenty years. Volunteers from the church head up various programs in the prison and serve as a resource to inmate-led small group Bible studies. Several times a year they get permission from the state Department of Corrections and Ark Valley to hold a "yard event" where they bring in a worship team, set up a stage, and Josh or another pastor preaches live in the prison yard.

They told me that "a ton of guys come out for that." Usually some of the Ark Valley inmates play in the worship band. When I inquired about the impact of the church's ministry there, I was told that "a bunch of guys were just baptized there last week!" And not only do they support the prisoners who are incarcerated, but they have an aftercare component with a statewide reach, actively helping individuals reintegrate into the community post-release. Ask those who are challenged with the task of overseeing Ark Valley and those in the Colorado correctional system who are battling high recidivism rates if they are thankful for the help of these Christians. They will say without hesitation that the impact of the work of WVC is significant.

Jesus' commitment to move into the lives of the "least of these" is evident when He tells His disciples that part of their credentials for being welcomed into His kingdom is, among other things, their care for prisoners. He says, "Come, you who are blessed by my Father, inherit the kingdom prepared for you from the foundation of the world. For I was hungry and you gave me food, I was thirsty and you gave me drink, I was a stranger and you welcomed me, I was naked and you clothed me, I was sick and you visited me, I was in prison and you came to me" (Matt. 25:34–36).

It's clear that Woodmen Valley Chapel has solid kingdom credentials empowered by *kalos* works that bring glory to God!

. . . .

The success of all of these ministries and others like them that are lighting the night of their communities and the world in the name of Jesus is due to a host of thousands of volunteers who have signed up to advance the kingdom agenda. And there are many as well who can't volunteer but who generously support ministries like these with their finances and prayers. These are the real heroes. These are the many who take seriously the stewardship of "this light of mine" and ignite the work of Jesus for His glory and the gain of His kingdom. Each of us has a light! I welcome you to use yours to light up the name of Jesus where you live. Being on the lookout for opportunities to love and express the love of Jesus in visible deeds of good works is what faithful light-bearers do.

Taking It Personally

Hundreds of thousands of women and girls are caught up in commercial sexual exploitation each year, and this is just in the United States. "I had no concept that women were being forced to sell their bodies on the same streets and in the same neighborhoods where I was raising my family and driving my kids to school," says Simone Halpin. Most of us would not have realized that. Simone's eyes and heart began to open to women being commercially sexually exploited when one night, she and several other Christian women went out to a street corner in Chicago and delivered gift bags to women caught up in prostitution.

Following God's leading, she eventually founded Naomi's House, a ministry for women trying to break the bonds of this lifestyle. One thing she is often asked is, "Why don't the women just leave? Why do they stay with those who pimp and exploit them?" She explains that "these traumatic experiences deeply impact how women see themselves and how they think God sees them—traumatic sexual abuse takes a lot of slow and intentional work to overcome." Simone continues: "When a woman comes out of the life of commercial sexual exploitation, the transition to caring for herself and allowing herself to be in the moment is so drastic that it can feel overwhelming." She tells of "Bea," who, in her mid-fifties, described how terrifying it was to *allow* herself to heal. For the first time in decades, she was choosing to trust God and enter into a healing journey that would set her on a path to a flourishing life if she embraced the help.

As Bea told Simone her story, she shared that the person who had encouraged her to come for help was herself a graduate of Naomi's House. "In our years of serving survivors, we are now seeing a ripple effect of survivors helping survivors," Simone affirmed. "This is why I started Naomi's House: every woman who has been commercially sexually exploited deserves a new start, and Naomi's House is here to help her find it."[33]

Lael Lemire is the site director at Hope Harbor in Minnesota, a nonprofit that provides hope and healing to at-risk teens.[34] She explains that for many, "the roots that eventually lead to being commercially sexually exploited stem from other places of deep wounding, trauma, and vulnerability from very early in life." Early on working with Hope Harbor she encountered "Myra." At just thirteen, this young teen had already experienced more pain than most people will in a lifetime. Myra grew up moving from state to state with her mother and siblings as her mother's drug addiction became more dangerous, eventually leading her mother to not only prostitute herself but also her children to get her next fix.

Lael continues, "At Hope Harbor, it took months before Myra would look anyone in the eye, or even smile. She believed she was too far gone for a second chance, and it wasn't until she gave her life to Jesus that we started to see true healing begin to take root. But healing is possible, no matter how deep the wound has been. Sometimes we encounter intensively heavy stuff, but seeing even one life changed and witnessing the healing makes such a difference."

Providing safe spaces to people who have been or who are at risk for being sexually exploited may seem overwhelming. "Working with survivors can be challenging," Julie Ipema acknowledges. Julie started Sheltered 91, which takes its name from Psalm 91:4: *Under his wings you will find refuge.* "People maybe think it can be kind of dark or scary, but it's actually really full of hope." She explains that trafficking survivors need specific, individualized care when they are ready to begin their recovery. She adds that in addition to those professionally trained for this ministry, other kinds of volunteers are needed who can help in "ordinary" ways, such as mentor, lead Bible study, be a driver, do administrative work, and teach life skills such as cooking or budgeting.[35]

Kalos bringing light to dark places. Being Jesus in a non-Jesus world.

. . . .

The late Paul Eshelman was well known for leading the Jesus Film Project. His desire was that every person on earth would hear at least one time that they were loved by God. Today the film is available in over two thousand languages, and hundreds of millions of people have seen it.

Paul had a great role in faithfully presenting Christ's love to an astonishing number of people but, while most of us will not have such a profound reach, everything a believer does for the kingdom is beneficial; we may not know this side of heaven how far-reaching our own *kalos* efforts will go.

Several years ago, Paul told me this story. He was meeting with a group of advertising moguls from a major Hollywood film company and discussing global marketing strategies for a new release of the Jesus Film.

In the room was the senior executive. He was someone with an immense profile in the movie industry and happened to be Jewish. When the meeting ended, this man asked Paul if he could take a moment to meet with him privately in his office. Paul was glad to comply.

The marketing executive told Paul about his life. At one point, he and his wife had faced a challenging health problem with one of their children. Around that time, he had seen their live-in housekeeper kneeling in her room in prayer.

Later, he had a chance to ask her about this. He wondered what she was praying about. The housekeeper replied, "I've been praying for your child, that God might be gracious and heal her." This woman continued, telling the executive that she had been praying for the child throughout the health crisis. Then she added that she prayed for the whole family every day.

Deeply moved, the film marketer asked if she would pray a blessing over him and his wife as they left for work each morning, and a daily habit began.

A few months later, another crisis hit the exec's family. This time it was his wife who was seriously afflicted with breast cancer. Her prognosis was not encouraging. Disheartened, one evening the executive walked down the street to find consolation at his synagogue. Discovering the building lit up and full of people as it was bingo night, he kept walking and soon found a church with its doors open.

Going in, he encountered the pastor in the sanctuary. This powerful man poured out his grief. The pastor listened, assured him of his concern, and prayed with him.

The next morning, when he went to visit his wife in the hospital, the doctor turned to him and said, "I thought you were Jewish."

"That's right, I am."

"Oh," the doctor replied. "Then why was a pastor sitting and praying at your wife's bedside throughout most of the night?"

As Paul Eshelman listened, deeply intrigued, the movie executive said, tears filling his eyes, "Our housekeeper passed away this week. And now I have no one to get me to God. Can you help me?"

Paul replied, "Can I tell you about Jesus?"

The executive said, "Of course!"

Before Paul left the office, the powerful mover and shaker had prayed to receive Christ as his Savior.

It was a humble, compassionate housekeeper who empowered the gospel by the good works of her love and prayers. And a faithful pastor who routinely loved as Jesus loved who brought this powerful executive to the cross. Paul, the pastor, the housekeeper . . . *kalos* love for the kingdom.[36]

Bloom and Flourish

Sometimes *kalos* is no more than everyday faithfulness. It is people who are observably different in a positive way. It comes from people who distinguish themselves as trustworthy and who make noticeable contributions to their businesses and community. It is acts of Christ's love, large and small, influencing your neighbor or influencing the culture.

Taking *kalos* personally is what early Christians did. What Chris Goeppner's church does. What Dan Cathy did. What Simone Halpin and others in this ministry do. What Steve Cochlan does. What I did in Starbucks. What a resident housekeeper did. What a pastor visiting the hospital did. And what you and I can do every day!

When I turned thirty-five, which is now ancient history, I remember getting a birthday card from my mother-in-law that said on the inside, "Bloom Where You Are Planted!" *Kalos* people bloom where they are planted for Christ and His kingdom! They are people who forgive quickly; love deeply; serve readily; labor honestly; act neighborly; clothe, feed, and nourish warmly; give generously; endure hopefully; stay steadfast courageously and embrace truth confidently . . . in other words, they are a lot like Jesus in a non-Jesus world.

Bursts of Light in Our Dark World

We will know that our light-shining lives are bringing dawn to the darkness when people around us start saying, "I don't get Christians, but our company is a far better place because of the ones who work here!" Or "I don't understand Christians, but our neighborhood is a better neighborhood because they live here." Or "I don't know what motivates Christians, but our school is a better school because they get involved!"

It's like Show and Tell. Remember? It's my favorite memory from kindergarten, next to naptime! In our world we will often have to win the attention of others by showing the ways of Jesus before we get the privilege of speaking up about Him. Of course, there are times when someone is ready to listen and we can readily share the good news with them. But for the most part, lighting our world with our good works opens the ears and hearts of those we rub shoulders with, giving us the opportunity to speak up. And when we shine His light, in time, even our worst enemies may want to hear about the One who made us this way.

It's no wonder that the writer to Hebrews exhorts brothers and sisters this way: "Consider how to stir up one another to love and good works" (Heb. 10:24). And it is notable as well that Paul calls followers to

Do all things without grumbling or complaining, that you may be blameless and innocent, children of God without blemish in the midst of a crooked and twisted generation, among whom *you shine as lights in the world.* (Phil. 2:14–16)

——————— **TO THINK ABOUT** ———————

In what ways will your life and your response to our culture be different as a result of what you have learned in this book? Would you be willing to honestly evaluate what your attitudes and actions have been like in contrast to living like Jesus in a non-Jesus world? Are you willing to prioritize the gospel and the advance of His kingdom above all other interests in regard to navigating the world we live in?

HAIL TO THE TEAM!

This Light of Mine is one of those books that is far better given the important contribution that wise and objective eyes have made to enhance its worth and value. A big thanks to my wife, **Martie**, who carefully reviewed the manuscript offering suggestions that took the ideas in this book to the next level. **Pam Pugh**, my lead Moody Publishers editor, made significant improvements and helped me think through the content from a reader's point of view. Her seasoned wisdom helped bring clarity and balance to the discussion of the topics at hand. I could go on, but suffice it to say, Pam's contributions were legion. Thanks as well to **Drew Dyck**, my acquisitions editor (aka "cheerleader"), who encouraged me to write this book in the first place and shepherded me through the publishing process from front to finish with wisdom and grace. And a big cheer goes to **Connor Sterchi** and the many others at Moody Publishers who labor behind the scenes to produce a useful finished product.

I am thankful as well for those who took their valuable time to review and endorse the message of the book. May their encouraging remarks draw many to read the book, bearing much fruit to their account.

A special thanks to those who through the years have influenced my life and thinking about the primacy of the gospel and the supremacy of Christ's kingdom. To these friends, professors, pastors, and colleagues; to our children with whom I have had engaging conversations about our King and His kingdom; to authors whom I have read . . . I remain a debtor. A debtor to the influence of their accumulated biblical wisdom that is now deeply engrained in my mind and heart regarding illuminating the darkness of our culture with the light of Jesus and His kingdom.

All of us who preach and write know the feeling of ecstasy when we have a thought that we think is brilliant. Only to wonder if perhaps, long ago, we heard that thought from someone who was far wiser than we are and have forgotten who, when, and where, thinking now that it is our own. So to all of those whose compelling thoughts and ideas have been planted in my soul and forgetful mind, thank you.

But most of all, I know that without the gifts that God has graciously bestowed on my life for His ministry; and without the many privileges with which His grace has favored me, especially the privilege of sharing life with Martie; and without His mercies that are new every morning . . . I would be nothing and incapable of writing anything worthwhile. Gratefully, I owe it all to Him! Soli Deo Gloria!!

NOTES

1. Dave Urbanski, "NBC Edits Out Christian NFL Quarterback CJ Stroud's Faith Proclamation Delivered During Interview After Playoff Victory," *The Blaze*, January 17, 2024, https://www.theblaze.com/news/nbc-edits-out-christian-nfl-quarterback-cj-strouds-faith-proclamation-delivered-during-interview-after-playoff-victory.

2. Francis Schaeffer (1912-1984), a Presbyterian minister, is often credited with providing an intellectual framework for evangelicals to understand their faith and engage thoughtfully with culture. His landmark book *How Should We Then Live?* was published in 1976.

3. J. R. R. Tolkien, *The Fellowship of the Ring* (New York: Ballantine, 1954), 93.

4. Ibid., 55–56.

5. "What Is an Evangelical?," National Association of Evangelicals, https://www.nae.org/what-is-an-evangelical/.

6. "US Adults See Evangelicals Through a Political Lens," Barna, Culture, November 21, 2019, https://www.barna.com/research/evangelicals-political-lens/.

7. Ibid., quoting David Kinnamon.

8. Will Carless, "After Convoy, 'Army of God' Rallygoers Filmed Themselves Harassing Migrants, Report Says," *USA Today*, February 16, 2024, https://www.usatoday.com/story/news/investigations/2024/02/16/texas-border-army-of-god-migrant-hunters/72621328007/. The participant was quoted as saying "We're illegal hunters. I've hunted a lot in my life, but I've never actually hunted people, and that's what we're doing now."

9. See David French, "A Critique of Tim Keller Reveals the Moral Devolution of the New Christian Right," *The Dispatch*, May 8, 2022, https://thedispatch.com/newsletter/frenchpress/a-critique-of-tim-keller-reveals/.

10. Kristine Parks, "Christian Pastor Dropped by Radio Network Stands by Advice to Grandmother on Attending LGBTQ Wedding," *Fox News*, January 30, 2024, https://www.foxnews.com/media/christian-pastor-dropped-radio-network-stands-advice-grandmother-attending-lgbtq-wedding.

11. The 2022 ruling in Dodds v. Jackson Women's Health is a landmark decision that determined the US Constitution does not protect the right to abortion. "The Constitution makes no reference to abortion, and no such right is implicitly protected by a constitutional provision," wrote Justice Samuel Alito for the majority.

12. *Choose Life: Answering Key Claims of Abortion Defenders with Compassion* (general editors Jeanette Hagen Pifer and John Goodrich) is a fine resource.

13. Paul McClure, "Reign Above It All," on *Revival's in the Air,* 2020, Reign Above It All lyrics @ Bethel Music Publishing, Essential Music Publishing.

14. "7 Joyful Truths about Following Jesus," Bible.com, https://www.bible.com/reading-plans/20757-7-joyful-truths-about-following-jesus/day/2. Also, from AI Overview: "The Greek word *akoloutheo* is used in the New Testament to mean 'to follow' 'accompany,' or 'to be a disciple of a leader's teaching.' It can also mean 'to imitate.' The word's primitive meaning is 'to walk the same road,' which is represented in the English word *acolyte.*"

15. Rebecca Paveley, "Evangelicals Not Popular in US, Says Survey," March 24, 2023, *Church Times,* https://www.churchtimes.co.uk/articles/2023/24-march/news/world/evangelicals-not-popular-in-us-says-survey.

16. Brian Keepers, "It's (Past) Time to Bury the Culture Wars," *Reformed Journal* (blog), May 28, 2022, https://blog.reformedjournal.com/2022/05/28/its-past-time-to-bury-the-culture-wars/.

17. "The Brand of Evangelicals: A Barna Briefing, 2019," https://access.barna.com/wp-content/uploads/2019/11/Barna_PerceptionsOfEvangelicals_WhitePaper_v6.pdf.

18. "Great Is Thy Faithfulness," Thomas O. Chisholm, 1923. Public domain. https://hymnary.org/text/great_is_thy_faithfulness_o_god_my_fathe.

19. You can find this wonderful organization at https://www.alsfamilyoffaith.center.

20. "Sing the Wondrous Love of Jesus," Eliza Edmunds Hewitt, 1898. Public domain. https://hymnary.org/text/sing_the_wondrous_love_of_jesus_sing_his.

21. Clare O'Connor, "Chick-fil-A CEO Cathy: Gay Marriage Still Wrong, But I'll Shut Up about It and Sell Chicken," *Forbes,* March 19, 2014, https://www.forbes.com/sites/clareoconnor/2014/03/19/chick-fil-a-ceo-cathy-gay-marriage-still-wrong-but-ill-shut-up-about-it-and-sell-chicken/.

22. Danica Coto and Jim Salter, "What We Know About the Young Missionaries and Religious Leader Killed in Haiti," Associated Press, May 26, 2024, https://apnews.com/article/haiti-young-missionaries-killed-gang-violence-ba69910971aaa0542233d6bd2a947d78#.

23. "Am I a Soldier of the Cross?," by Isaac Watts, 1724. Public Domain. https://hymnary.org/text/am_i_a_soldier_of_the_cross.

24. I also contrast *agathos* and *kalos* in *I Would Follow Jesus* (Chicago: Moody Publishers, 2005).

25. Philip Jenkins, "How Many Christians?," *Patheos.com*, September 27, 2017, https://www.patheos.com/blogs/anxiousbench/2017/09/how-many-christians/. Jenkins is citing *The Rise of Christianity* by Rodney Stark.

26. "Edict of Milan," *Britannica*, https://www.britannica.com/topic/Edict-of-Milan.

27. "Constantine I, Roman Emperor, *Britannica*, https://www.britannica.com/biography/Constantine-I-Roman-emperor/Commitment-to-Christianity.

28. Quoted in John Piper, *A Godward Life: Seeing the Supremacy of God in All of Life* (Colorado Springs: Multhomah, 2015), 253.

29. I write about these events in *The Trouble with Jesus*, drawing on Rodney Stark's book *The Triumph of Christianity*.

30. Will Durant, *The Complete Story of Civilization* (New York: Simon & Schuster, 2014), 602.

31. "This Little Light of Mine" is an African American song written in the 1920s. It was later adapted and sung during the civil rights movement. Public domain.

32. Shannon Najmabadi, "Midsize Cities Struggle with Snowballing Homelessness, *The Wall Street Journal*, December 20, 2023, https://www.wsj.com/us-news/midsize-cities-struggle-with-snowballing-homelessness-5f15536f.

33. You can find out more about Naomi's House at naomishouse.org. Some of the material in this account is taken from "Hope Lives Here" by Linda Piepenbrink, December 31, 2001, https://www.moody.edu/stories/grad/2021/hope-lives-here/.

34. Learn more about this ministry at https://www.hopeharbormn.org.

35. You can find out more about Sheltered 91 at sheltered91.org.

36. I also tell this story in *The Trouble with Jesus*.

Lord, give me strength.

The Christian life is a journey filled with mountaintops and valleys. This enriching devotional overflows with thought-provoking questions and keen biblical insights. Stowell encourages us to consistently turn to the Word of God for sustenance on this lifelong pilgrimage. Your faith will be nourished and refreshed.

Also available as an eBook

You finished reading!

Did this book help you in some way? If so, please consider writing an honest review wherever you purchase your books. Your review gets this book into the hands of more readers and helps us continue to create biblically faithful resources.

Moody Publishers books help fund the training of students for ministry around the world.

The **Moody Bible Institute** is one of the most well-known Christian institutions in the world, training thousands of young people to faithfully serve Christ wherever He calls them. And when you buy and read a book from Moody Publishers, you're helping make that vital ministry training possible.

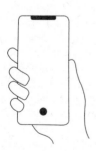

Continue to dive into the Word, *anytime, anywhere.*

Find what you need to take your next step in your walk with Christ: from uplifting music to sound preaching, our programs are designed to help you right when you need it.

Download the **Moody Radio App** and start listening today!

 MOODY Publishers® 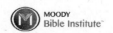 MOODY Bible Institute™   MOODY Radio®